Participants celebrate completion of the Parent Project, Kagel School, Milwaukee.

A Family History Project,
Allen Field School, Milwaukee.

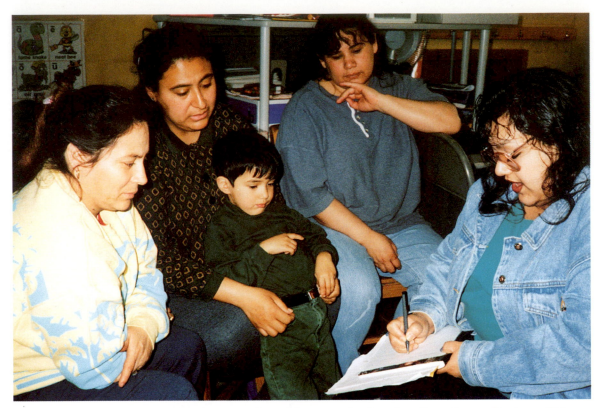

Parents explore new ways of solving math problems in the Pritzker-Burr Parent Project, Chicago.

Parent Crystal Vega prepares for the Parent Literature Circle Project, Stockton School, Chicago.

More Than Bake Sales

More Than Bake Sales

The Resource Guide
for Family Involvement in Education

JAMES VOPAT

Carroll College, Waukesha, WI
Director, Milwaukee Writing Project

Contributions by Pete Leki

S

Stenhouse Publishers

York, ME

Stenhouse Publishers, 431 York Street, York, Maine 03909
www.stenhouse.com

Library of Congress Cataloging-in-Publication Data
Vopat, James.
      More than bake sales : the resource guide to family involvement in
   education / James Vopat ; contributions by Pete Leki.
         p.   cm.
      ISBN 1-57110-083-0 (alk. paper)
      1. Home and school—United States—Handbooks, manuals, etc.
   2. Education—Parent participation—United States—Handbooks,
   manuals, etc.   3. Community and school—United States—Handbooks,
   manuals, etc.   I. Leki, Pete.   II. Title.
   LC225.3.V67   1998
   371.19'2—dc21   98–24867
                                                              CIP

Cover and interior design by Geri Davis, The Davis Group, Inc.
Cover photograph by James Vopart
Cover art and interior icons by Laura Hermann
Typeset by Octal Publishing, Inc.

Manufactured in the United States of America on acid-free paper
03 02 01 00 99   9 8 7 6 5 4 3 2

This book is dedicated

to the foundations that have supported the Parent Project:

the Faye McBeath Foundation, the Milwaukee Foundation,

the Annenberg Foundation, the W. K. Kellogg Foundation,

the Helen Bader Foundation, and especially

The Joyce Foundation of Chicago.

Contents

Author's Note

You are invited to adapt and refine the workshops in this book in whatever ways you find helpful and, of course, to develop your own.

Since it is the intent to honor the voice of workshop participants—parents, children, and teachers—their writing is presented as it was received with no further editing.

Acknowledgments

To Jacqueline Ward, Bama Grice, Pete Leki, Pat Bearden, Yolanda Simmons, Dave Gawlik, Mark Schimenz, Rebecca Borjas, and Toby Curry for helping give shape to this book; To fellow Walloonatics Smokey Daniels, Steve Zemelman, Marilyn Bizar, Nancy Steineke, Barbara Morris, Toni Murff, and Mary Hausner; To Barbara Kines for her encouragement and helpful commentary; To Cross City Campaign for Urban School Reform for their insistence on community/school collaboration; To Philippa Stratton, Tom Seavey, and Martha Drury—

This book wouldn't exist without all of you.

Chapter 1

"Where Are We Going?" First Let Me Tell You About Where We Have Been

Art by Ajala Hughes, from Parent Project publication "The Incredible Illustrated Biopoems," Hi-Mount School, Milwaukee.

*T*he Parent Project began in Milwaukee in the late 1980s as a way of involving parents more intentionally in their children's education. The project was a five-year collaboration between Title I directors, teachers, social workers, parents, and parent coordinators in the Milwaukee public schools. Together, we developed a number of workshops designed to support parent and teacher partnership centered on the classroom curriculum—including such activities as reading, writing, critical thinking, and creative dramatics. When parent concerns surfaced, we designed workshops around these issues as well—from self-esteem to fire safety. The story of how the Parent Project developed (along with its workshop formats) was told in *The Parent Project,* published by Stenhouse in 1994.

Since 1994, thousands of parents and teachers have participated in Parent Projects in a wide variety of locations—urban, suburban, rural, big city, small town, elementary, middle, and high school, community centers, and teacher training and parent leadership institutes. Their experiences have affirmed many of the principles that originally guided us, and have helped us develop new ways of connecting school and home—all for the benefit of children. This book records the new journeys we have been on, the directions taken, the parent voices heard along the way.

In 1996, the Parent Project was named by the U.S. Department of Education as one of six Parents as First Teachers national models as part of President Clinton's "American Reads" Challenge:

> Responding to the thirty years of research showing the importance of parental involvement both at home and at school in a child's school success, the goal of the . . . Project is clear: increasing parental involvement, building a bridge between parents and teachers, and focusing on improving the achievement of children. . . . Teachers and parents meet in weekly workshop where they discuss the literacy work being focused on during the school day and develop a home "application" that parents can use to work with their children at home. The parents try to use the application (i.e., journals etc.) during the week and discuss its success in the workshop the following week. Groups meet weekly for 6 weeks, then monthly. The program tries to identify and recruit committed parents who can serve as group co-leaders.
>
> The Program has been able to document its impact through data on attendance, referrals, and performance on state-testing. In Beloit, Wisconsin, for example, by the end of the first year of the program, parent involvement had increased 128%. In the Hi-Mount Elementary School, Dr. Jerome Blakemore of the University of

Wisconsin-Milwaukee found that there was a 66% reduction in school suspensions for children of project parents and an 82% reduction in behavioral problem referrals. Tardiness reports for children whose parents were involved in the program declined almost 400%. (Clinton 1996, p. 25)

What the Department of Education description doesn't convey is the quality of interaction between parents and teachers—which is inventive and enthusiastic when focused on children's learning. The quality of this parent-teacher interaction I hope will emerge from the chapters of this book.

Four principles have guided our work with parents and teachers:

1. Parents are not only their child's first teacher, but are also an ongoing teacher and lifelong influence.

2. Parents and teachers share the same goal: the academic success of children.

3. There is no reason to separate parents and teachers when it comes to the education of children. Working equally and together, parent and teacher can increase each other's understanding and enrich the learning of children.

4. Engaging parents and teachers in writing and reading workshops not only builds a sense of community but also renews an enthusiasm for learning.

"Strong parent involvement is not a question of 'Should we?' but rather a question of 'How should we?'" Regie Routman writes in *Invitations* (1991, p. 485). First, though, we should ask "What is 'parent involvement?'" Doesn't its definition greatly influence the answer to "How should we?"

The Milwaukee Public School District publishes an annual report on school progress for each of the system's 163 schools. Each school's report includes a "School Narrative," which highlights goals and programs. For 1996–97, all but about 25 of Milwaukee's schools included a paragraph or two under the heading "Parent Involvement." Activities and programs mentioned included, but were not limited to: cookie sales, raffles, family fun nights, breakfast with dads, mentor programs, playground carnivals, exercise classes, GED programs, Parent-Teacher Organizations, playground duty, parent-teacher conferences, clerical help, committee meetings, participation in School Decision Making councils, parenting classes, field trips, computer classes, book fairs, Title I meetings, open houses, guest speeches, ESL courses, coffee chats with the principal—even taking care of the school pet.

The roles for parents and families engaging in these activities are varied. They can be volunteers, fund-raisers, audience members, decision makers, and advocates—with limited opportunities in decision making. Parent involvement is most commonly viewed and reported in numbers; parent involvement is apparently greatest for parent-teacher conferences and special events.

There is a sense in reading through the various descriptions of parent activities listed by the Milwaukee public schools that a distinction can be made between parent "participation" and parent "involvement" in school. Not that there is anything wrong with cookie sales, or playground duty, or any other way of helping schools better educate children. If the purpose of parent involvement is to help children do better in school, however, there needs to be more opportunities for parents to connect in meaningful and intentional ways with the classroom curriculum and teachers. Indeed, it is possible for a school to have a number of well-attended special events and still fail to make the essential connection between school and family. As one Milwaukee School Narrative expressed it: "Our active parent group does not reflect the school population's racial and cultural diversity."

Given the questions they ask and their enthusiasm to experience learning along with their children, it seems that parents' interest in how they can interact and support classroom instruction is often underestimated and therefore underutilized. A 1997 survey by Milwaukee's Public Policy Forum asked 270 Cleveland and Milwaukee parents, teachers, and school administrators to indicate what mattered most in a school. The most common parent response (59 percent) was the "school program"; while only 15 percent answered "test scores" (*Milwaukee Journal Sentinel*, Nov. 12, 1997, p. 1). Surveyed parents' most frequent answers to what was important in choosing a school for their children were as follows:

School program (59 percent)

Teachers (45 percent)

Outcome–general (35 percent)

School characteristics (31 percent)

Safety and discipline (28 percent)

Outcomes—test scores (15 percent)

Parent involvement (12 percent)

Reputation of schools (9 percent)

The fact that parents were most often interested in information about the school's program, primarily its curriculum and method of instruction (p. 1),

"I want to help to get my child an education so that he can make it when he leaves school."

validates our workshop experiences and perhaps helps explain why parents are not drawn to school activities that they perceive as peripheral to what really matters: the education of their children.

Try this brief visualization:

When you think about "parent involvement" in your school what kinds of things come to mind? Where do you see this involvement happening?

This is what *More Than Bake Sales* is about: expanding the definition of "parent involvement" and how it occurs. We begin with a description of the Mighty Acorns Parent Project as a demonstration of the workshop approach. We then explore elements that contribute to the success of the Mighty Acorns Parent Project. We'll hear the Legend of the Bright Blue Bush and learn about Parent Projects that focus on family history, literature circles, academic standards, and leadership. We'll listen to parent voices and celebrate what others have accomplished as we work together to reclaim the family-school connection.

WELCOME.

Chapter 2

Caution—Parent Involvement Ahead: The Mighty Acorns Parent Project

Parents and students at Whittier School in Chicago planted native forbs and grasses in the school garden as part of the Mighty Acorns Parent Project.

*S*heila Epstein, a teacher at Chicago's Whittier School, made the following
observations about the Mighty Acorns Parent Project:

> It was wonderful seeing the parents exploring, learning, and hav-
> ing fun. I was able to participate in most of the weekly sessions, and
> I usually was there to hear the parents share their writing. Their
> writings were filled with interest, involvement, humor and love.
>
> The parents explored the neighborhood and investigated things
> of interest to them. Sometimes they would look at the different types
> of trees growing within the community, while other times they had a
> deep desire to learn more about the garbage along the Chicago River.
> Always there was interest in what they were doing, and they would
> write about their feelings and findings. They were excited to share
> their writing, and were eager to hear the other parents read aloud.
> As time went on there was a stronger sense of community growing
> within the parents.
>
> On a personal note, I think the meetings, interaction, and learn-
> ing going on within the group was a beautiful thing. As an educator,
> it was extremely exciting to see the parents posing questions, investi-
> gating, researching, writing, and sharing the same way their children
> do. They were able to experience learning in a hands-on experience,
> something most of them were not familiar with when they went to
> school. The culminating experience was when they went to Cap
> Sauers Woods and were able to see and touch all the things their
> children have been doing for the past year.

Mighty Acorns is a program of the Nature Conservancy and the Cook County
Forest Preserves. The goal of Mighty Acorns is to give children hands-on experience investigating their immediate environment, the prairies, and the wood-
lands. Since Mighty Acorns had been an established ecology curriculum at
Whittier School for a number of years, it seemed a timely and, yes, natural way
to involve parents and the community in the school.

Wanting parent involvement is one thing; achieving it, however, is
another. For various reasons—including illness, timing, the weather, and the
demands of work—it was difficult to recruit a sufficient number of participants
for the Mighty Acorns Parent Project.

In order to spark enthusiasm for parent involvement in Mighty Acorns,
Whittier students and teachers decided to put on an evening's entertainment.
A notice went out to parents of third-, fourth-, and fifth-grade students invit-

ing them to attend a "kid created" show about the students' experience at Cap Sauers Forest Preserve and at the nearby Laflin bank of the Chicago River. "The students hope to teach parents about these two ecosystems as well as gain parents' support to help clean up the river site," the invitation read. "Parents can learn more about how our students learn by joining the Parent Project."

Students in the three grades worked together building stage sets, making masks, composing music, choreographing dances, and writing scripts. Entitled "Trip to Cap Sauers," the resulting "kids' show" was more like a two-act musical. Act One opened to a scene of a typical Whittier classroom a few days before the field trip. Students reenacted their own questions and fears, from the mundane ("Are there bathrooms in the forest?") to the philosophical ("Can I put seeds in my pocket to take back to school?"). The scene then shifted to the day of the trip and the announcement "THE BUS IS HERE!"

Act Two took place in the forest itself, re-creating the sights, sounds, and inquiry through bilingual dialogue, dance, and music:

DAVE: What are these squishy brown things?
ARTEMIO: They are walnuts. Let's pick some up and crack them open.
DAVE: These walnuts are hard to crack open.
DEB: Just keep trying, like this.
GUS: Oh these are good.
NOE: Yo siento feliz porque es muy bonito en el bosque.

DANCE

"Trip to Cap Sauers" was a great success. It served as a demonstration of learning by the students, increased parents' understanding and enthusiasm, and resulted in more than the envisioned number of parents being ready to embark on their own Mighty Acorns Parent Project.

While the Mighty Acorns Parent Project was designed to give parents the experience and information necessary for them to understand a major school curriculum (ecology), the nature of the project also encouraged parents to model a spirit of inquiry, community involvement, and sense of ownership of their natural environment. The Mighty Acorns program for Whittier students depended on the recruitment of parents as docents to lead school groups; an additional benefit of the Parent Project would be a larger corps of informed and enthusiastic parent docents for student field trips to Cap Sauers.

FIRST SESSION

Welcome
Paired interviews
Creating a group portrait
Read-aloud: The Big Rivers *by Bruce Hiscock*
At Home journal activity: write or draw "Rivers of Our Homelands"

The Mighty Acorns Parent Project was facilitated by Pete Leki. Pete was originally a parent participant in a Parent Project at Chicago's Waters School, and now worked full-time developing Parent Projects in Chicago. Pete welcomed the participants and briefly described the goals of the Mighty Acorns program. Participants were given name tags and journals. The journals would be used to write and/or draw responses and reflections during the weekly sessions. The journals would also be a convenient way of keeping track of the weekly "At Home" activities designed to connect the Mighty Acorn Project with other family members.

Parents began by interviewing each other and then introducing the person they interviewed to the rest of the group. The interview questions were designed to move the participants from personal information to questions about homeland landscapes, native plants, and what the Whittier neighborhood might have looked like more than a century and a half before, in 1830. The four interview questions reflected the Whittier School community and were presented in both Spanish and English:

1. Name, place of birth.
    Nombre, lugar de origen.
2. Describe the landscape of your homeland.
    Explica como es la tierra o paisaje de su tierra nativa.
3. Name a plant or animal native to your country of birth.
    Nombra una planta o animal nativo de su tierra.
4. How do you think this neighborhood (around Whittier School) looked 160 years ago?
    Explica como era nuestro barrio hace 160 años.

The interview question asking how the Whittier School neighborhood might have looked 160 years before provoked a lot of interest and a variety of opinions, from "pure dirt" to "desert" to "few houses" to "full of trees." Pete showed participants an 1830 land map of the area, which depicted the site of Whittier School as an oak woodland abutting the unobstructed waters of the Chicago River. The area was called Pilsen.

Using information from the paired interviews, and combining details from their respective homelands, everyone helped generate a group portrait. The result was poetic, a kind of historic-panoramic landscape sweeping from Chicago to Mexico:

The Landscapes, Los Paisajes

sierras, mountains,
ranchos, ranches
lagunas, ponds
praderas, grasslands
Lake Michigan with the lights of the city
80 degrees, warm in winter, mummies, dry soil
dryness, seco, beaches, playas, Rumorosa
Fruit trees, where the Mexican flag originated
Montañas, mountains, coolness, little villages
Many trees and flowers
Houses all the same, except the colors
Very rich, water, anamargo, alfalfa; in a valley surrounded by mountains
Peaceful, green with lots of agriculture, mountains
Very green, lemon trees, mangos
Había piedras, burros, verde

A read-aloud of Bruce Hiscock's picture book *The Big Rivers* furthered participants' general interest in the natural environment while eliciting even more enthusiasm for the home journal activity: to write or draw whatever was suggested by the phrase "Rivers of Our Homelands." *The Big Rivers* was about the Missouri, the Mississippi, and the Ohio rivers, and specifically the disastrous floods of spring 1993. The book concluded with an "Author's Note" in which Hiscock recounted the three trips he made to the rivers in order to write his book and how he "began to see how complex our environmental issues have become."

In the week between the first and second sessions, lists of parents' maps showing their birthplaces, journal reflections about indigenous plants and animals, and the "The Landscapes, Los Paisajes" group portrait were prominently displayed in the main entrance to Whittier School. The display would grow and change with each weekly Parent Project meeting, honoring the project while also keeping the greater Whittier School community informed about its progress (see photo).

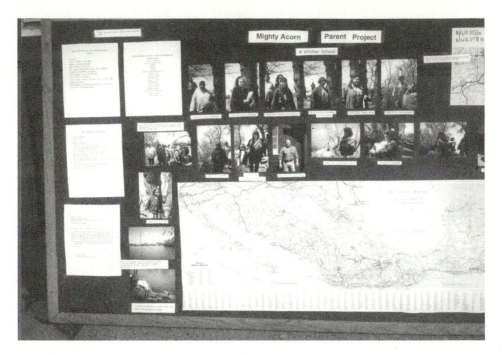

The Mighty Acorns Parent Project display at the entrance to Whittier School kept students, teachers, and the rest of the school community up to date about the weekly workshops.

SECOND SESSION

Welcome
Sharing: "Rivers of Our Homelands"
Read-aloud: The Little House by Virginia Lee Burton
Journals: A walk in the neighborhood
At Home: Draw a representation of our neighborhood

The next week, the Mighty Acorns Parent Project participants regathered, sharing news of the week and the journal writing about homeland rivers. The journal writings, such as the one by Elisa Rodriguez (Figure 2.1), tapped evocative distant memories.

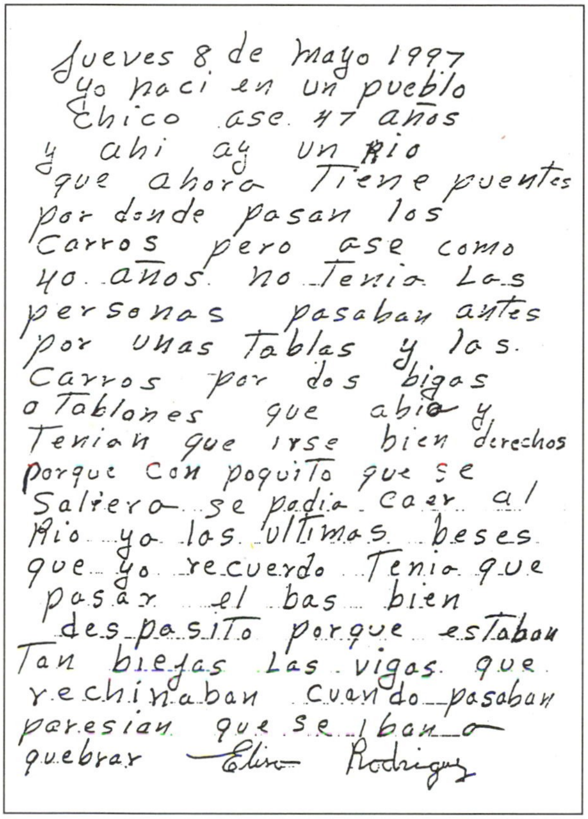

Jueves 8 de mayo 1997
Yo naci en un pueblo
Chico ase 47 años
y ahi ay un Rio
que ahora Tiene puentes
por donde pasan los
Carros pero ase como
40 años no Tenia Las
personas pasaban antes
por unas Tablas y los
Carros por dos bigas
o Tablones que abia y
Tenian que irse bien derechos
porque con poquito que se
Saltera se padia caer al
Rio yo los ultimas beses
que yo recuerdo Tenia que
pasar el bas bien
despasito porque estaban
Tan biejas Las vigas que
rechinaban cuando pasaban
paresian que se iban o
quebrar — Elisa Rodriguez

Figure 2.1   Elisa Rodriguez's journal entry "Rivers of Our Homeland."

Thursday, May 8, 1997

I was born in a little town 47 years ago, and there is a river there that today has bridges that cars pass through. But about 40 years ago it didn't have any bridges. People would walk over on wooden boards and cars would cross over on large beams and they had to cross very straight. If they were to deviate a little they could fall into the river. The last time I recall the bus had to pass very slowly because the beams were so old that they creaked when one would pass through, as if they were going to break.

Originally published in 1942, Virginia Lee Burton's picture book *The Little House,* our read-aloud for the second session, presented a deceptively charming chronicle of urbanization and change. The story was told from the point of view of a house in the countryside as it experienced the seasons, technological change, and population explosion. Inevitably, the little house became surrounded by a polluted and noisy metropolis looking a lot like Chicago—complete with elevated train. Seasons disappeared in the grime and noise as the skyscrapers rose until the little house "only saw the sun at noon." At the story's end, the little house was rescued from the urban congestion, moved to another idyllic, distant, countryside location, and restored.

Pete's read-aloud of *The Little House* put everyone in an adventurous mood as they readied themselves to explore the Whittier neighborhood. The walk in the neighborhood, journal in hand, turned members of the group into close observers of the immediate physical environment. People wandered off in pairs or groups, or by themselves; the only requirement was to return at the specified time with some observations or drawings in the journals. Diane Reckless's "Neighborhood Walk" (Figure 2.2) captured the sense of adventure in spite of (or because of?) the blustery cold Chicago weather.

Figure 2.2　"Neighborhood Walk" finds the sun snoozing.

After returning to the school, parents shared observations in small groups. Perhaps because of the story of *The Little House,* many found themselves contrasting present-day Chicago with the idyllic wooded scene depicted in the map from 1830. The At Home journal activity to be done during the coming week was inspired by the neighborhood walk: participants were to draw a representation of the neighborhood.

THIRD SESSION

Welcome
Sharing: Maps of our neighborhood
Guest speaker from Friends of the Chicago River
Field trip to the Chicago River origin site
At Home: Share journal impressions of Chicago River with family

The big surprise the next week, when the neighborhood maps were shared, was the absence of the Chicago River. Once majestic and an essential part of the landscape, it was now nowhere to be seen (as in Ms. Pacheco's map, Figure 2.3).

A guest speaker from the conservation group Friends of the Chicago River provided a brief history of the river, particularly of the local river site. This was good preparation for the field trip to the Chicago, the neighborhood's own "Big River." Children joined their parents on this field trip to the nearby Laflin riverbank, and single-use disposable cameras were available for photo documentation. Participants were asked to photograph whatever struck them as important as they toured the badly damaged and polluted river site. As people walked along the riverbank, various members of Friends of the Chicago River helped them imagine the river and its bank as a healthy and restored ecosystem. Parents wrote in their journals and photographed their impressions.

The At Home activity was for everyone to share their journal entries, their impressions of the field trip, with other members of the family.

Figure 2.3   Neighborhood as seen by Ms. Pacheco. Notice that the Chicago River is nowhere to be seen.

FOURTH SESSION

Welcome
Writing about photographs
Guest presentation: Nature Conservancy
Small-group work: Selection of native plant for school garden
Read-aloud: This House Is Made of Mud/Esta casa esta hecha de lodo *by*
 Ken Buchanan
At Home: Write a short poem or prayer to share as you plant your native species

At the fourth session, the photographs of the river site had been developed, and parents introduced themselves by talking briefly about why they chose to photograph what they did. All the photographs focused in some way on the environmental damage that years of pollution, dumping, and neglect had wreaked on the river site.

Writing and then sharing observations about the photographs reinforced everyone's determination that something had to be done to reverse the environmental damage. Under his photograph of brush and plastic scraps, broken glass, and wires in what looked like a gravel-strewn garbage dump, Miguel Miranda wrote:

Look at these plants. They are trying to grow here but the trash is stopping it from growing. There are tire scraps and other things so look closely, as hard as you can. Look! Look at that. Do you hope it get better again? Keep this picture in your heart so you can know it's ugly.

After hearing Miguel and other parents read, the group decided to include their photographs and impressions as part of the ever-enlarging Parent Project display at the Whittier School entrance.

The session's guest speaker, from the Nature Conservancy, talked about restoration of native ecosystems and plant habitats. Everyone then ordered a native plant from the nursery catalogue, to be planted in the Whittier School garden during the next session.

Written by Ken Buchanan and illustrated by Libba Tracy, the read-aloud of *This House Is Made of Mud/Esta casa esta hecha de lodo* depicted an isolated mud house that also came to represent the family, the world, and the universe. Through the metaphor of the mud, the book underscored the interdependence of home and natural environment.

The At Home activity was for everyone to write a small poem or prayer to share with the group as they planted their native species during the next week's workshop.

FIFTH SESSION

Welcome
Journal sharing with children
Planting activities
At Home: Select writing/drawing for publication
Read-aloud: la primavera *by Asun Balzola and Josep MaParramon*

Children joined their parents for the fifth session, so some reintroduction of parents, now with their children, was in order. The native species plants in small plastic pots had arrived and were distributed. A renewed sense of reverence towards nature was evident as parents shared their poems and prayers for these plants with their children. Maria Rico's piece "The Plants" was written in Spanish:

> Luz y alegría es lo que refleja tu verde follaje,
> Algunas frondobas otras pequeñas, pero todas con un
> Sólo objetivo, embellacer al planeta.
>
> Paz, amor y mucho cuidado es lo que necesitan y pronto
> Las veremos en su llenas de flores y hojas
> Algunas necesitaran más cuidado, más agua pero
> Nadie se quedará sin proteccion porque a
> Todos las trataremos y les daremos todo el cariño y
> Amor que se merece para que se desarrollen y
> Se vea nuestra escuela como la mejor del mundo.

> Light and happiness is what reflects from your green foliage,
> A few with big leaves others with small ones, but all with a
> Single objective, to beautify the planet.
>
> Peace, love, and much care is needed and soon we'll
> Look and see you grow with your great gala of flowers and leaves
> A few need more care, more water but
> No one is left without protection because all are
> Treated and given great care and
> Affection that is deserved so that all can grow and our school will be
> Seen as the best in the world.

Rosa Valdez also wrote in Spanish (see Figure 2.4); a translation of her poem "Hojas" (Leaves) is given below:

My color is so beautiful and clear,
Green is my color,
I fill myself with the heat of the sun
during the pretty afternoons
My leaves are large and narrow,
Such that I always want to fly
To capture the pure air that
my arms long to ask for.

The rest of the session took place in the school garden, where parents and children recited their poems as they planted the native species, helping to beautify the Whittier School environment—to quote parent Maria Rico, "so that all can grow and our school will be/Seen as the best in the world."

Hojas

Mi Color es tan bello y claro,
Verde es mi Color,
Me lleno del Calor del sol
en las hermosas tardes,
Mis hojas son largas y Angostas,
Que Siempre quiero Volar
Para Capturar el aire Puro que
mis brazos suelen Pedir.

Figure 2.4   Rosa Valdez, "Hojas" (Leaves)

Precisely because *la primavera* by Asun Balzola and Josep MaParramón conveyed the sense of seasonal growth and new beginnings, it provided an especially appropriate read-aloud.

Since the next week's meeting would be the last scheduled workshop, everyone was encouraged to look through their journal and select what they wanted to include in the Mighty Acorns Parent Project publication. Parents and teachers could also decide to write something new.

SIXTH SESSION

Welcome
Sharing of selections for Mighty Acorns publication
Evaluation, certificates, stipends
Celebration!
Read-aloud: Amorak by Tim Jessel

Parents and children again met together for the final session, and parents began by sharing what they had chosen to represent themselves in the group publication: poems to rivers and native plants, neighborhood maps, illustrated stories about homeland rivers, and many pleas for environmental protection and restoration of the Chicago River. The most striking aspect of the writings for publication had to do with the way the parents connected the well-being of the environment with the nurturing of their children. Sr. Raquel Ahmad's poem "Las Flores" (The Flowers) provides an example of this connection:

> Las flores y las plantas
> Cuando empiezan a crecer
> son como capullos
> que van abriendose
> con el rocío de la noche
> Cuando les platica uno les gusta
> son como los niños
> les hablamos con amor
> y crecen bellas.
>
>
> The flower and the plants
> When they start to grow
> are like cocoons
> that are opening
> with the dew of the night
> When one talks to them, they are

> like children
> we talk to them with love
> and they grow beautifully.

While very modest ($30 per individual), participant stipends served to acknowledge the time commitment required by the project. (For more information about stipends and funding see Chapter 3.)

Evaluation forms were printed in Spanish and English. Parents were asked to note what they liked and didn't like about their experiences in the project, as well as suggestions for follow-up. *Amorak* by Tim Jessel is a retelling of an Inuit legend about the interdependence of all life and served as a fitting read-aloud for the final session of the Mighty Acorns Parent Project.

The concluding celebration was marked by storytelling, plans for follow-up meetings, group photographs, good food, and a sense of pride of accomplishment.

FOLLOW-UP

There were three follow-up activities. The first was a field trip to Cap Sauers Woods for a walk and tour. Children accompanied their parents, and together they not only heard about but also experienced environmental restoration techniques.

The second follow-up was occasioned by the distribution of the Mighty Acorns Parent Project publication. Publication was, as always, a fine reason for a celebration and author's party. Many parents read their stories and poems aloud. The public reading was accompanied by frequent exchanges of the publication for autographs and brief written commendations.

The third follow-up activity occurred when parents joined their children in writing letters to the Metropolitan Water Reclamation District of Chicago requesting that the MWRD clean up and safeguard the local river site. The letters (translated into English where necessary) were sent to the attention of the MWRD:

> *People of the River,*
>
> In the most attentive form, I direct myself to you to ask you, and if necessary to beg you, to clean up and take care of the river, since it is a precious jewel that nature offers us. It would be wonderful to beautify it, through cleaning and planting, and taking care of its trees; it could be a marvelous view not only for the community but for those who come to visit the city. It would be very degrading and very sad that all of these people that visit the city take away a bad impression.

On the contrary, with your support and help the city would be beautified and would be another part of Chicago to admire, visit, and take walks with family so that the community and its visitors can be proud.

Waiting for a positive response and your unconditional support, and with that, sending greetings from a group of parents interested in rescuing the nature of the city.

Your sure and attentive server,

Maria Rico
Parent Project

To Whom It May Concern,

My name is Elisa Rodriguez and I write you this letter to give my opinion on how I would like the river to be. I think that the river should have more access to the public, and if they could have explanations as to why the river is important to all of us. It would look beautiful if it was clean; I think that it would be much benefit if the river could be clean because people would notice it more since there are people that don't even know about it.

I would like for you to consider my opinion and I am willing to cooperate with the clean-up as much as I can.

Elisa Rodriguez

Whittier parent and student letters resulted in the MWRD's undertaking a major cleanup of the Laflin Street site along the south branch of the Chicago River. Through the Mighty Acorns Parent Project, parents, students, and teachers—working together—not only connected home and school, family and curriculum, but also managed to get the Laflin Street site cleared of mountains of rubbish. Project participants also began planning how to transform the river area into a nature preserve and water studies laboratory.

"Parent involvement takes work. It doesn't just fall out of the sky."

Currently, Whittier students and parents are helping to design and maintain a new park commemorating the I&M Canal, which connects the Great Lakes to the Mississippi.

The Mighty Acorns Parent Project may initially seem difficult to replicate. In fact, however, the essential components are not that unusual. They are: a facilitator who is comfortable with the workshop process; appropriate guest speakers;

As part of the Mighty Acorns Parent Project, parents pull
garlic mustard, an invasive alien weed, to free up the native
wildflowers.

and a classroom or school curriculum sufficiently vital to sustain the interest
of parents. The Mighty Acorns Parent Project was successful because it
emerged from the Whittier School curriculum–and, indeed, served to deepen
and extend that curriculum. It is also important to recall that it was the enthusiasm of the children (through the "Trip to Cap Sauers" play) that provided the
initial motivation for parents to participate.

WHAT YOU CAN DO

Here's what you can do to initiate a Parent Project:

1. Select a significant aspect of your classroom curriculum and/or
    teaching practice that will benefit from parent input and ownership—
    a thematic unit, perhaps, or a writing workshop; the creation of math
    manipulatives, or the issue of computer literacy; whatever seems
    appropriate. Like good picture books, authentic learning will hold
    interest for parents as well as students.

2. Invite parents to a series of workshops in which they will be able to
    experience the particular curriculum or classroom practice. As with
    the "Trip to Cap Sauers" play, utilize student enthusiasm as a means
    of recruiting parent participants.

3. Identify other teachers, community members, or parents who can make guest presentations as part of the parent workshops.

4. Allow the interest and enthusiasm of participants to give direction to your efforts, continually focusing on how parents' experience with the classroom curriculum will enable them to support and promote their children's learning.

Chapter 3

"Looks Like a Lot of People Having Fun, but What Makes It a Parent Project?"

Parents enjoy children's picture books at Stockton School's Parent Literature Circle Project, Chicago.

A Parent Project contains the following elements:

- *Workshop sessions*. Parent Projects usually involve a manageable number of parents and teachers meeting in regular, experiential two- to three-hour sessions. The focus of the workshops should reflect the interests of the participants and should include hands-on interaction and the construction of home activities (described below) that extend the information and learning into the family environment.

- *Leadership*. Someone has to conduct the workshops. Ideally, this "someone" is a parent-teacher team. Because this book describes a workshop approach to parent involvement, it can be seen as leading up to the chapter on leadership (Chapter 10) subtitled "It Doesn't Happen Just Because You Say So."

- *Sharing*. The group re-forms at the beginning of every meeting in a way that avoids anyone's being left out or unheard. Often this means giving everyone an opportunity to share the results of the home activities devised in the previous workshop. Individuals who missed the previous meeting or did not try any of the home activities are still welcomed and made part of the group by being invited to share some "news."

- *New information*. Each workshop meeting has a clear focus, which often involves a short presentation (often by school staff or a parent) on a subject chosen by participants.

- *Home activities*. Whatever the workshop focus, parents and teachers enjoy brainstorming how they can extend their experience into the home and community. When dealing with the classroom curriculum, parents are especially interested in what they can do to support their children's learning. Parents use their journals to record the results of home activities with their family.

- *Firsthand experience*. Workshop activities give participants the experience of reading, writing, doing math, performing science experiments, and so forth rather than just talking about them. Having parents and teachers work in small groups and pairs helps bring a sense of collaborative purpose.

- *A supportive atmosphere*. A quiet place, tasty snacks and drinks, child care and translation facility if needed: these things greatly increase the chances of a Parent Project's being a powerful group experience. Parents and teachers are important. We need this time and space to build our community.

- *Book reading*. Reading favorite books out loud to each other reminds us what a good feeling it is to be read to. It also helps expand the range of reading choices for everyone. Some Parent Projects have circulating libraries so participants can check out books each week and then report back to the whole group on great books as well as "duds."

- *Journals*. Journals become diaries, photo albums, art books, family treasures. Each week parents find reasons to write and share at home with their children. And children get the message: writing is important, an everyday activity, and fun. Writing is to be enjoyed, not corrected; parents who are uncomfortable with writing are encouraged to draw and/or work with a "scribe."

- *Fun*. People learn better in communities where trust has been built and a relaxed supportive atmosphere exists. Our job as facilitators of Parent Projects is to be good models of empathetic listening, bringing everyone into the group—writing, reading, and sharing.

- *Children at the center*. Quality education for children is what brings parents and teachers together.

- *Flexibility*. When dealing with the worlds of school, home, and community, you've got to be flexible. This means acknowledging and adjusting to issues and concerns of participants as they arise.

- *Stipends*. Whenever possible, we provide stipends to participants, facilitators, and guest presenters. Stipends for participants in a typical six-session Parent Project range from $30 to $150 per individual for all six sessions. Stipends are a way of acknowledging that parents incur costs as a result of their participating, for such things as transportation and additional child care expenses. Stipends also signify that we value the time and commitment of parents as they participate in the weekly workshops and complete the various home activities. Funding for stipends and other expenses comes from a variety of sources—individual school budgets, grants from foundations, and Title I. (For more information about Title I, see the question-and-answer section, Chapter 12.)

- *Publication*. Writing generated by the Parent Project should be made available to the entire school and the community at large. Such pieces are valuable documents about the history of the community and a great way to model writing for a larger audience. If there is one thing that characterizes our approach to parent involvement, it is the publication of parent writing. Parent Project publications often involve collaboration between parent and child, as was the case with the piece shown in Figure 3.1, from the "I Remember" publication of Milwaukee's Engleburg Elementary School Parent Project.

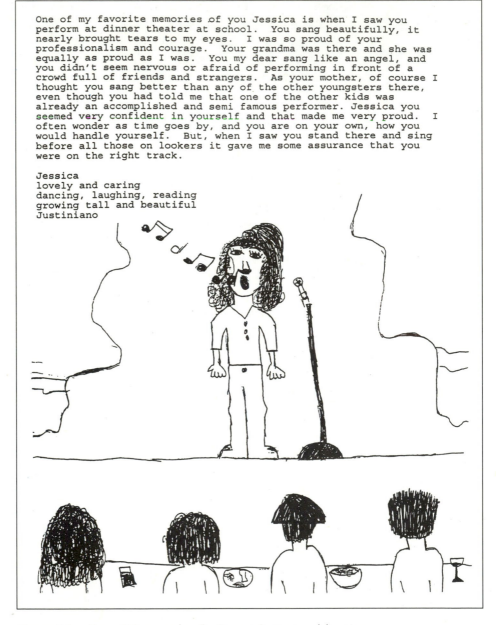

One of my favorite memories of you Jessica is when I saw you perform at dinner theater at school. You sang beautifully, it nearly brought tears to my eyes. I was so proud of your professionalism and courage. Your grandma was there and she was equally as proud as I was. You my dear sang like an angel, and you didn't seem nervous or afraid of performing in front of a crowd full of friends and strangers. As your mother, of course I thought you sang better than any of the other youngsters there, even though you had told me that one of the other kids was already an accomplished and semi famous performer. Jessica you seemed very confident in yourself and that made me very proud. I often wonder as time goes by, and you are on your own, how you would handle yourself. But, when I saw you stand there and sing before all those on lookers it gave me some assurance that you were on the right track.

Jessica
lovely and caring
dancing, laughing, reading
growing tall and beautiful
Justiniano

Figure 3.1   From "I Remember," a Parent Project publication from Milwaukee's Engleburg Elementary School, by Jacqueline and Jessica Ward.

WHAT OTHERS ARE DOING

Rebecca Borjas, an elementary school teacher in Santa Maria, California, conducts home visits as a way of introducing herself to her students' families. The home visits allow Rebecca a greater understanding of how to teach her students and give her a sense of individual parents' expertise and the ways parents can enrich her classroom curriculum. Rebecca arranges the home visits by sending a notice home with her students, explaining the purpose of the visit. Parents return the notice, indicating convenient times and dates for the visit. The home visits take about half an hour, and Rebecca's interview questions help define the potential resources of her classroom community. (Rebecca's home visit notice and interview form are included in Appendix C.)

"We parents never get a voice to be heard."

WHAT YOU CAN DO

Survey the parents of your students as to the times they are available to meet and the kinds of issues they would like to focus on in a workshop. Check to see if there are funds available for stipends and expenses, either in the school budget or through Title I. Feeling adventurous? Contact local foundations and request a copy of their annual report. The annual report should give you an indication of whether the foundation would be interested in funding parent involvement initiatives. In writing grant applications, emphasize how the project will contribute to the students' academic success. Collaborating with other teachers and parents in your funding endeavor makes the effort more manageable and increases the likelihood of receiving funding. Searching out funding for parent involvement initiatives can itself be a powerful form of community building.

Chapter 4
Community Building

Community building at Allen Field's Family History Parent
Project, Milwaukee.

We spend time and energy on community building in Parent Projects for many reasons. There is often some initial mistrust between teachers and parents, tension between home and school. There is, as well, always a feeling of awkwardness when people who do not know each other well come together. That the place we gather is often a school setting can increase the discomfort, especially for those who have had negative school experiences.

At the same time, parents and teachers have the same goal: the well-being of children. Parents and teachers have every reason to work together, and every reason to break down the barriers—often artificial—between them. Ideally, many of the activities in a Parent Project workshop will establish and strengthen the sense of community. Every time we meet with parents and teachers, the general success of the meeting depends on whether we begin with an activity that strengthens our sense of community. To *welcome* participants to a weekly Parent Project workshop is to repeatedly re-form the group and strengthen the bonds between participants.

Community-building activities are entertaining and usually give participants an opportunity not only to work together, but also to (re)introduce themselves to the entire group. Slowly we begin to learn names and connections to schools and what is important to people. When asked what is necessary to improve the relationship between home and school, parents and teachers repeatedly answer "trust" and "communication." Through community building, we are able to gradually establish this trust and communication, while also getting to know each other. The more long-term the parent involvement—be it curriculum projects, shared governance, or leadership—the more necessary the community building becomes.

There are a number of successful ways of building a sense of community, and what you choose depends on the group's participants and purpose. Community-building activities that involve people working together to solve problems are especially effective for leadership training sessions in which groups of parents (often from different schools) learn to facilitate Parent Project workshops (see Chapter 10).

There are four primary ways of re-forming a group after some days or weeks have elapsed since the last meeting:

1. *Reporting on progress.* Participants report on family activities suggested by the previous week's workshop.
2. *Using "boundary breakers."* Participants respond to a provocative and interesting question or activity.
3. *Solving problems.* A problem is presented to the whole group and participants work together to solve the problem and then reflect together and individually on the process.

4. *Conducting interactive read-alouds.* Children's picture books can often be used to focus everyone on the workshop agenda. Becoming a member of the audience for a memorable read-aloud is a community-building experience in and of itself. If the read-aloud also involves interactive elements—predictions, role playing, reader response—it serves the Project on a number of levels.

PROGRESS REPORTS

The beginning of each workshop is crucial because it sets the tone for the rest of the time spent together. Progress Reports are especially important if there are home activities to be tried between Parent Project meetings. For example, when participants decide to take their children to a library during the week to check out a book, everyone at the next meeting will want to know how it went and will want to validate their experiences with the other members of the group. If it has been an interesting home activity, the progress reports will take up as much time as you allow them to. Workshop leaders are often impatient to get on with the agenda, but the time spent savoring the results of home activities not only validates the activities but centers everyone on the main goal: how families can support student achievement in school. At the least everyone needs to be given some time to comment on the week's home activity. It is through these commentaries that options for family involvement are clarified. The cumulative experience of participants informs everyone as to the range of choices before them.

BOUNDARY BREAKERS

Boundary breakers are aptly named because they encourage everyone to provide new information about themselves. The best boundary breakers are relevant to the current workshop focus. A boundary breaker about favorite places will almost always produce interesting results ("Think of a favorite place—a place you always look forward to visiting. When we go around and introduce ourselves this evening, tell us one of the places you thought about"). But such an opening provocation becomes much more meaningful when it is connected to the rest of the evening's agenda—for example, the opening of an environmental workshop. If there is an art to running Parent Projects, it has to do with giving continuity to the various activities. Boundary breakers can exist solely as a way to introduce members more intimately to each other, but they are more powerful when they simultaneously deepen understanding of the workshop focus.

A fail-safe Parent Project boundary breaker is to ask each person to share some school or family news from the previous week. Since the overriding purpose of the boundary breaker is to promote a sense of community, it is important that everyone have information to share.

Once you begin to see boundary breakers as nonjudgmental ways of learning more about participants while also engaging them in the beginning of an inquiry process, numerous possibilities come readily to mind:

- *Name stories.* "Tell us something about your name. How do you feel about your name? Do you have a nickname? Who are you named after? Did you change your last name when you married? Do you have a middle name?" Name stories not only help participants remember everyone's name, but they give the group a number of interesting glimpses into family history. Sandra Cisneros's chapter "My Name" from *The House on Mango Street* provides an encouraging and poetic read-aloud: "In English my name means Hope. In Spanish it means too many letters" (1991, p. 10).

- *Treasure Hunts.* In this activity, the group facilitator makes a list containing something that is true for each participant, leaving the person's identity blank. (An example of such a list is shown in Figure 4.1.) He or she then hands out copies of that list and a list of the participants' names. Once the lists are distributed, participants work in pairs to match names with personal details. This is another way for participants to learn names and understand individual interests and expertise. Identifying information for the Treasure Hunt often comes from previous introductions or interviews of participants (thus also giving participants a sense that they have been listened to). More than one name sometimes applies to a given characteristic. This is fine; in fact, it helps bring people together.

- *"If I could . . ." questions.* "If I could be a character in a book I would be . . ." (for a session on reading); "If I could travel anywhere in the world, I'd travel to . . ."; "If I could live one day of my life over, the day I would choose would be . . ."; "If I could pick one talent, it would be . . ."

- *Who, what, where, when, why questions.* "Who is the most important person of our time?" "What event of the last three months stands out in your mind?" "What will you be doing ten years from now?" "What future discovery are you looking forward to the most?"

PROBLEM SOLVING

Problem-solving activities are actually mini-workshops in and of themselves. Problem-solving activities usually involve participants in group work and reflection, and are most appropriate when a group has been working together for a few weeks. Many of the Milwaukee public schools have a "Ropes & Challenge" curriculum in which students become involved in physical activities

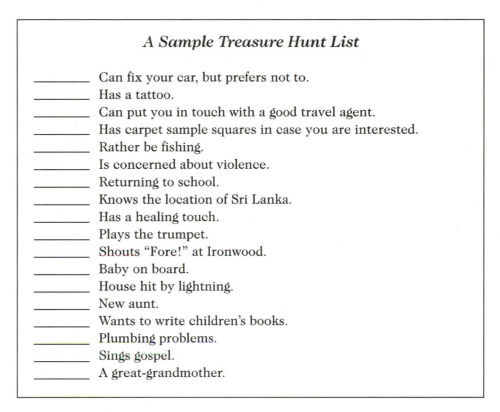

Figure 4.1   A Sample Treasure Hunt List

as a way of promoting teamwork. In the Parent Project, we try to utilize learning strategies institutionalized in schools and districts, especially if these strategies are unfamiliar to parents. Ropes & Challenge problem-solving activities not only brought Parent Project participants together in a cooperative way, but also allowed everyone time to reflect on the meaning of community.

In one Ropes & Challenge Parent Project workshop, Milwaukee middle-school counselor Mark Schimenz had us think about what goals we, as a group, wanted to accomplish. Mark then had each of us blow up a balloon and write his or her goal on the balloon. Each person shared the goal, and it was interesting to discover the commonalties. Mark then led us in a demonstration about how we might support the group's goals as well as our individual goals. We would be given the goal balloons one at a time and would have to keep all of the balloons in the air at the same time. It was up to us as a group to figure out how we were going to accomplish this. After trying out a number of formations (close circle, loose circle, inner circle/outer circle) we were finally able to keep all the balloons airborne—if only briefly. After the group reassembled, Mark led us in a discussion of how we felt about the activity and what we learned. Repeatedly teachers and parents mentioned the need to work together, to have a plan, to be nonjudgmental, and to not give up. Not only had we arrived at important group principles, we had also gained a sense of individual priorities—and we had fun!

READ-ALOUDS

Diez Deditos (Ten Little Fingers), selected, arranged, and translated by José-Louis Orozco and vibrantly illustrated by Elisa Kleven, is a particularly effective community-building read-aloud. *Diez Deditos* is a collection of thirty-four finger rhymes and action songs in Spanish and English. The songs can all be sung by groups and are enjoyed by young children and adults alike. The majority of the songs involve participants in physical activity—especially important for workshops that begin in the evening when everyone usually is tired. Other particularly effective community-building read-alouds include Sandra Cisneros's *Hairs = Pelitos*, Faith Ringgold's *Aunt Harriet's Underground Railroad in the Sky*, and Tomie dePaola's *La Leyenda del Pincel Indio*.

"We knew we had to include everybody, and we spent time figuring out how to do that."

Though you will occasionally encounter individuals who dislike activities they dismiss as being "touchy-feely," there is, in the Parent Project, every reason to encourage touch and feeling. If the home-school community is not built and repeatedly strengthened, meaningful interaction cannot occur. Community building may seem time-consuming at first. The time spent, however, should be considered an investment that will make group activities and decisions much easier and forthright in the long run.

In a Parent Leadership Project workshop (see Chapter 10), we reached the following consensus about community building:

- *It has to happen*—not only at the beginning of the workshop, but as part of every activity.
- *Take time*. Because of its democratic nature, there is never enough time to accomplish everything any one workshop will set in motion. Community-building activities usually involve every participant, and therefore can take a lot of time that could be spent conveying information. *Take the time*. If the community has not been formed, the information will not have its full effect.
- *Focus*. One way of dealing with the time limitations and the numerous community-building activities that could be chosen is to be clear about the

focus of the workshop. Ideally, the community-building activity not only will be compatible with the workshop's focus, it will also help to narrow and advance the workshop's agenda.

- *There is something harmonious about sitting in a circle*. What is a community if it's not a circle?
- *Reflect*. What does this experience mean? Why go through the effort unless there is something to learn and enjoy? Continually in the community-building activities we try to set aside even more time (!) to talk about what has been learned. Parent Projects are a time for reflection. What have we learned about our primary reason for coming together—the education of children?

One observer at a Parent Project workshop mentioned afterward that she couldn't tell the parents from the teachers, a comment that we took to mean that our community-building activities were a success.

Each time Mark Schimenz concluded a Ropes & Challenge activity, he would ask us to place the palm of our right hand down and our left palm up, connecting palm to palm with the person on either side of us. "We are all equal," he would say. "No one is above or below anyone. We are all equal as we work for the well-being of children."

WHAT OTHERS ARE DOING

Part of community building involves gaining the ability to approach issues from perspectives other than your own. In other words, teachers must think like parents; parents must think like teachers. In an article in the *Middle School Journal,* Patrick Renihan and Frederick Renihan point out that parents should not be held accountable to rigid definitions of "ideal" involvement: "We see ideal involvement rather as a process, one which gives parents the opportunity to invest and divest depending upon such changing factors as the school level of their own children, their own working schedules, and changing family patterns" (1995, p. 58). The Renihans also suggest that schools and teachers offer "several levels of involvement, thus free[ing] parents to 'buy in' to the school at their own level of comfort and as their own circumstances dictate" (p. 61).

WHAT YOU CAN DO

Build the agenda of your project from the interests of the participants. This can be done as part of your inaugural community-building activity. Pair participants and have them interview each other, not only about personal information (ages and grade levels of children, hobbies) but also educational interests and school concerns ("What made you want to participate in this workshop?" "What aspects of school and learning would you like us to focus on as a group?"). Have individuals introduce the person they interviewed to the rest of the group. Keep a list of interests and concerns. If there is an overriding issue that emerges, follow it.

RESOURCES FOR COMMUNITY BUILDING

Donald R. Glover and Daniel W. Midura. 1992. *Team Building Through Physical Challenges*. Champaign, IL: Human Kinetics

Daniel W. Midura and Donald R. Glover. 1992. *More Team Building Challenges*. Champaign, IL: Human Kinetics.

Terry Orlick. 1996. *The Second Cooperative Sports and Game Book*. Dubuque, IA: Kendall Hall.

Chapter 5

Enlarging the Literature Circle

Crystal Vega and her reader response journal, Parent Literature Circle Project, Stockton School, Chicago.

*D*uring the initial meeting of the Parent Project at Chicago's Stockton School, facilitator Pete Leki led participants in a brainstorming session focusing on parent concerns. The following questions were listed:

- How do we keep our kids in school, prevent their dropping out?
- How do kids see their parents? What do kids like and dislike in their relationship with parents and adults?
- How can you talk to your children so that they can believe you, trust you, stay close to you?
- How can we keep our kids off drugs?
- How can our oldest children help (relate to) the younger ones?
- How do I get involved in my child's education? How can we schedule ourselves to be part of our children's school?
- How can we improve parent-teacher communication?
- How can we help our kids and our school confront and overcome racial prejudice?
- What would it mean for our school to become bilingual?

Clearly a six-week Parent Project could not handle this range of issues, but it could begin the process in a meaningful and collaborative way. In Parent Project workshops one issue leads to another, especially when parents are involved in activities that acknowledge the principal connection between home and school: quality education for children.

At Stockton School, students in many classrooms were involved in literature circles, and parents decided that they wanted to experience literature circles as well. The plan that quickly developed was to organize the parent literature circles around the same group of adolescent novels that the parents' children were reading and discussing in Stockton's classrooms. The objectives were twofold: to give parents an understanding of how literature circles work through having them experience the activity themselves; and to engage parents and their children in ongoing dialogue centering on adolescent literature. In the process children would observe their own parents reading—in and of itself an influential factor in helping them develop the practice of lifelong reading.

The ensuing Parent Project was modeled on the structure defined by Harvey Daniels in *Literature Circles: Voice and Choice in the Student-Centered Classroom* (1994):

Literature circles are small, temporary discussion groups who have chosen to read the same story, poem, article, or book. While reading each group-determined portion of the text (either in or out-side of class), each member prepares to take specific responsibilities in the upcoming discussion, and everyone comes to the group with the notes needed to help perform that job. The circles have regular meetings, with discussion roles rotating each session. When they fin-ish a book, the circle members plan a way to share highlights of their reading with the wider community; then they trade members with other finishing groups, select more reading, and move into a new cycle. Once readers can successfully conduct their own wide-ranging, self-sustaining discussions, formal discussion roles may be dropped. (p. 13)

The Parent Literature Circle Project began with an introduction of the concept, which has become easier now that Oprah Winfrey has popularized book discussion groups through her daily television program. At Stockton School, where many of the participants' first language was Spanish, Pete read a selection from Saint-Exupery's *The Little Prince* in Spanish and in English, and then asked parents to write or draw a response in their journals. Parents were encouraged to jot down any thought or association that the passage brought to mind. After about five minutes, participants exchanged journals with a partner who briefly responded, again through writing or drawing. Next, as members of the group shared their brief paired dialogues, Pete noted the dif-ferent kinds of responses on the blackboard: one parent drew a picture, three connected the reading to everyday events in their lives, others made predic-tions about the rest of the book, still others focused on specific passages and events. In short, the parents' responses pretty well covered the range of liter-ature circle roles as defined by Daniels (pp. 76–104):

- *Literary luminary (iluminador de la literatura):* This person identifies a selection of text that has special meaning.
- *Illustrator (artitsta):* This person draws a picture related to the reading.
- *Connector (conector):* This person makes connections between the read-ing and the real world.
- *Summarizer (capitan de los personajes):* This person prepares a brief summary of the reading.
- *Word finder (sabelotodo de las palabras):* This person makes note of spe-cial words in the reading.

The one reading response role that did not emerge from the parents' dialogue journals about *The Little Prince* was modeled by Pete as he guided the discussion:

- *Discussion director (director/director(a) de la charla):* This person guides the discussion about the reading and helps the group decide on how much to read before the next literature circle session.

While it was interesting for parents to understand and participate in the various reader response roles, the crucial role for a book discussion meant to last over a series of weeks is that of discussion director. Pete explained that the discussion director role would shift from week to week, as parents decided in advance of each week's session how much they would read and what kind of role response they wanted to take on. Parents were encouraged to take on more than one role. What distinguished the Parent Literature Circle Project structure was that parents were to share their literature responses with their children at home.

After defining the possible reading responses and the role of discussion director, Pete began forming the literature circles themselves. He held what he termed a "Book Fair" in which he introduced the range of book choices to the parents. Pete had multiple copies of four young adult novels to choose from: Virginia Euwer Wolff's *Make Lemonade*, Sandra Cisneros's *The House on Mango Street* (or, in Spanish, *La Casa en Mango Street*), Camille Yarbrough's *The Shimmershine Queens*, and Esmeralda Santiago's *When I Was Puerto Rican*.

Pete gave a brief book talk about each title. Then, a fifteen-minute break for food and conversation provided parents with an opportunity to look through the book choices themselves. After the break Pete asked everyone to find at least two others who wanted to read the same book. And thus the parent literature circles began.

From week to week Stockton parents met to discuss the portion of their chosen book they had agreed to read. Much of the discussion turned to the conversations parents had with their children about the reading. Some parents read their book with their children, and some had their child read the book to them. Stockton parent Maria Aguilar was a member of the *Make Lemonade* literature circle. Her weekly reading responses were written down for her by her daughter:

> This book Make Lemonade relates to my life in similar ways. This Jolly that the narrator talks about is only 17 yrs. old and is a mother of two kids. She struggles through the whole book, no parents to help her out and the babies father is never there. The only person there to help her out is her 14 yr. old babysitter the narrator LaVaughn. This relates to me because I was also a young mother. I didn't have anybody but my mother. I knew that my mother could

not be there for me always. I had to leave my children in Mexico and move to the U.S.A. to find a good job that will pay good so I could send back to my children and be able to bring them here as soon as I was settled in. If I had brought them along with me I would be so afraid that they would take my children away from me, because I had no money for a baby-sitter and knowhere to stay just like Jolly.

(Maria)

I think this book is so amazing. It makes you really think how hard it is out there in the real world. How hard it is for a teenage mom having no parents to help her out and no babies father to help or pay child support. Also being so afraid that the welfare people might come and take your kids away because you don't have any-body to take care of your kids to go to work, and if you don't go to work you don't get paid, you don't get paid you don't have money to pay for anything. So this teaches you about something. It teaches you that it isn't easy out there, and if you do think it is easy just read this book and you will see that it isn't. This is a good book.

(Maria's daughter)

The parent literature circles continued to meet for four weeks. When the sessions came to an end, parents kept the copy of the book they read. It could become part of the family's home library and serve as a focus for dialogue with other family members in the future.

A field trip to a large bookstore in downtown Chicago was an appropriate and appealing way to celebrate the conclusion of the Parent Literature Circle Project. Parents and their children browsed through the bookstore in order for each to select a book, which the project was able to purchase through a small grant. Then parents and children sat in the bookstore

"I can't help at home if no one tells me what I need to do."

coffee shop sharing their new books over coffee, soft drinks, and pastries. Pete distributed the project publication, which contained excerpts from the parents' literature circle journal responses. This distribution of the participants' own publication prompted a spontaneous and enthusiastic author's book signing party.

And what about the brainstormed list of parent concerns that began the Stockton Parent Project? When we revisited the list of concerns after the experience of the parent literature circles, we found that inroads had been made on every one. The problems had not been solved, but the journey had certainly begun.

WHAT OTHERS ARE DOING

The following are some other kinds of literature programs that bring parents and children together.

- "Family Matters" is a six-week program that brings at-risk youth together with an adult family member to talk about books that relate to everyday family life. The program, sponsored by the Maryland Humanities Council, takes place in a variety of sites including community centers and homeless shelters. The purpose of the program is "to encourage a tradition of mealtime discussions" about books. Each family receives a free set of books. Once a week families come together for a dinner discussion of the readings led by librarians. At the conclusion of each six-week session, participants from all Family Matters sites gather to meet a guest author.

- Gallistel Reading Pals is a parent tutoring program at the Gallistel Language Academy, Chicago. In the program parents come to the school twice a week to read with two or three students for 40 minutes. The students choose the books they want to share with their adult Pal. Reading Pal sessions occur during the school day as well as after school. Reading Pals are trained to be model readers by Designs for Change, an educational research and reform agency in Chicago. (For more information regarding Designs for Change, see Appendix A).

- In her piece "A Delightful Journey: Literature Circles in First Grade" (Hill et al. 1995) Christy Clausen describes a process in which her first-grade students bring home a book every Friday of each week. Each child self-selects a book. The idea is for the child to read the book to his or her parent or for the parent and child to read the book aloud together. Parents are encouraged to talk about the book as they read, to read the book once or twice each night, and to have their children use stick-on notes to mark passages they want to share and talk about in class. Children return the books to school on Monday with the pages flagged. Clausen also provides parents with suggested questions that can be used to promote talking about the book.

WHAT YOU CAN DO

The following is a brief guide which you can use in developing your own Parent Literature Circle Project.

First, *introduce the idea*:

- Talk about book discussion groups—or, better yet, watch a tape of one of Oprah's reading discussions. Have parents say which books they and their children are reading.
- Generate the different literature response roles by conducting a brief read-aloud and discussion, then talking about the ways parents responded.
- Have students who are already participating in classroom literature circles demonstrate them for the parents.
- Have multiple copies of books that are appropriate and of interest to both parents and their children. Is it possible to use books that the children are reading in school?
- Make sure that the book selections reflect the languages of the participants.

Then, *properly manage the sessions*:

- Literature circles need to meet for at least three weeks.
- After being given a sense of the options, parents form literature circles around a book of their preference. ("Find two or three other parents to read your book with during the next few weeks.")
- Participants agree in advance of each week's literature circle session how far in the book they will read and the role they will perform in the group.
- Parents record their reading responses in their journal, often in collaboration with their children.
- Responsibility for being discussion director—as well as the other roles—rotates from week to week.
- If a parent doesn't get the reading done for a given session, he or she should still be welcomed by the literature circle members. (Even those who haven't done the reading can take the role of summarizer.)
- Give each literature circle time to share important points of their discussion with the entire group.
- Each session should include discussion of how parents have included their family in their weekly reading response.

Finally, *follow up*:

- Publish a booklet of parents' responses to their chosen books and distribute the booklets to the parents and their children.
- Establish dialogue journals between parents and their children centering on classroom reading.
- Invite parents to participate in classroom literature circles.

RESOURCES

Harvey Daniels. 1994. *Literature Circles: Voice and Choice in the Student-Centered Classroom*. York, ME: Stenhouse.

Bonnie Campbell Hill et al., eds. 1995. *Literature Circles and Response*. Norwood, MA: Christopher-Gordon.

David Laskin and Holly Hughes. 1995. "A Brief History of the Reading Group in America." In *The Reading Group Book*. New York: Penguin.

YOUNG ADULT NOVELS

Sandra Cisneros. 1994. *La Casa en Mango Street* (Spanish translation of *The House on Mango Street*). New York: Vintage.

———. 1991. *The House on Mango Street*. New York: Vintage.

Esmeralda Santiago. 1993. *When I Was Puerto Rican*. Reading, MA: Addison-Wesley.

Virginia Euwer Wolff. 1993. *Make Lemonade*. New York: Scholastic.

Camille Yarbrough. 1989. *The Shimmershine Queens*. New York: Putnam.

Chapter 6
The Roving Parent Journal

This is my family!

THEY ARE GREAT!

by Sontaine. Slaughter, Age 11

From "Becoming Us" Parent Project publication, Dewey Center for Urban Education, Detroit.

Dear Parents,

Welcome back for a great new school year. Thanks to all of you in advance for reading our class syllabus and returning the parent response sheet.

This year I am going to circulate this journal among all of my parents. A parent-teacher dialogue journal is a great place for us to talk about schooling, parenting, and kids. I'm a parent too. My children are 14, 16, and 18.

This journal will be a place for us to discuss any questions or concerns that you have about school. It is also a great way to keep the lines of communication open between school and home. Please let me know about any questions or topics you'd like to write about.

To get our conversation going, why not tell how you like the idea of a "roving parent journal."

And so Detroit sixth-grade teacher Toby Curry begins her ongoing dialogue with parents at the Dewey Center for Urban Education, a Detroit public school. The Roving Parent Journal is a simple yet sturdy spiral-bound notebook that passes, or "roves," from parent to parent over the course of the school year. "Whose mom or dad really likes to write?" Toby asks her students as a way of initiating the first journal entries. When a parent responds in the journal, Toby writes back in the journal and also makes a copy of her response to be sent home to the parent. The results are two ongoing conversations: one between the individual parents and the teacher; and the other a larger, collective dialogue of Toby's classroom parents. As the journal entries accumulate, parents inevitably read through earlier exchanges with other parents before writing their own, often referring to comments from previous parent letters and Toby's responses, and frequently using previous parent letters as a model for the form of their response. Once the journal has roved for a while, the audience for the letter exchanges comes to include the entire classroom community, and the opening salutations of the letters grow more expansive, from "Dear Ms. Curry" to "Dear Ms. Curry and Parents" and "Hello parents and Ms. Curry."

Through their letters, parents introduce their family not only to the teacher but to the larger classroom community, a community that is re-formed and strengthened with each letter exchange. The Roving Parent Journal, Toby says, especially appeals to parents whose hectic lives don't allow school visits. As you read the following dialogues between Toby and the middle school parents, notice how—as Toby would put it—the "Rah, rah, we love Ms. Curry" quickly develops into important insights about classroom curriculum and learning.

Dear Ms. Curry & Parents

My name is Dawn Bentley. My husband is Kevin and our son is Kevin II. I was so inspired by reading through the journal. It is a fantastic idea. I'd like to give a standing ovation to the parents as well as Ms. Curry.

My son Kevin has attended Dewey for five years and I was very thrilled to know that Ms. Curry would be his sixth grade teacher. I had observed her many times in the hall and I noticed that many interesting things were going on while passing her classroom. Kevin was excited as well, which was the most important response.

During the course of the semester I have truly noticed a wonderful change in his love for learning. Normally I asked him what he learned in school. Now he talks about many of the concepts learned freely.

My concerns regarding his schooling is handling conflicts in a non violent manner. Please give me some feedback on the subject.

I look forward to meeting you personally (we spoke on the phone a few times). It's a little difficult this year because I have two other children four and seven. My daughter Jasmine is at Dewey and my son Darryl is at another school.

May you all have a wonderful holiday.

Sincerely,

Dawn S. Bentley

P. S. I'm very impressed with the wonderful job that you're doing by teaching the children about different cultures. It helps them to respect individual differences as well as cultural differences. Something very important in our changing world.

Dear Ms. Curry:

I would like to express my deepest thanks to you and the staff of the Dewey Center. I am Kevin's father. I am involved in his life everyday. All too often fathers are not in the home of their children and it is a tragic situation for all involved. My wife and I love our children as well as other children and we have made careers in helping others. I visit the Dewey Center often and I see the struggle that you and your co-workers go through every day. It takes a great person to do that type of work. Teaching is like being a preacher in my opinion. A person have to be called to the job by a deep love for themselves and others. I am also very impressed with the wonderful job you are doing.

Thank you very much,

Kevin Bentley, Sr.

Dear Mr. and Mrs. Bentley,

It was wonderful that you *both* took time to write in our parent journal. I'm so glad that you got it over Christmas break so you could take some time to read through it. You've given me so many topics to respond to that I didn't have the time last week to give your entry the attention it deserved. I do apologize for making you wait a whole week to hear back from me.

I was so pleased to hear your discussion of Kevin as a learner over the years. It reaffirms for me that as parents we are our children's first teachers and we have the real longitudinal study of our children as learners. I loved your description of Kevin's "love" for learning. It has been truly delightful to see Kevin take on his research topics this year and share what he has learned with others. When he presented Japan last week he gave us some wonderful insights into Japanese culture and life. I could hear Kevin's "voice" come through loud and clear throughout his presentation.

When I look at the problems in our city and our world, I think you are very astute to pin point conflict resolution as one of the most important lessons we can teach our young people. I think this, like Mr. Bentley indicated, is directly related to the comfort, security and nurturing that children get at home. As many parents have written in this journal, raising children alone is a daunting task. So many of our single parents have dedicated their life and all of their resources to making a safe way in the world for their children. It's a hard job with two parent households, when there's only one parent present it is truly neverending. I have found the voices in our journal to be an inspiration to me as a mother. We have a group of "student conflict resolution" counselors in our room to help mediate conflicts that aren't too serious. Right now, two of Kevin's classmates have written a play on "conflict resolution" that they are going to perform for the 4th and 5th grade classes next semester. As Mr. Bentley observed, teaching children how to handle their conflicts and responses is something our whole staff must deal with on a daily basis.

Mr. Bentley, you are so right with your analogy about "teaching and preaching." They are both a "calling" to do a very special kind of work. I feel so fortunate to have found my true career (or calling) in life. I do love working with children.

Sincerely,

Toby Curry

Hello parents and Ms. Curry,

My name is Stephanie Rice and I am Kristen Marshall's mother. I have one other daughter and her name is Alexandra, she is 6 years old (or 6 1/2 as she will tell you) and she also attends Dewey. I was just telling Kristen prior to receiving this journal that I thought she was having a much better year than last year. Last year was our first year at Dewey and we experienced a lot of fighting and bickering amongst the students and we also had a bad experience with a couple of students and Kristen. My concern for my daughters is that in this world of crime, sexual assaults, and abject violence, that they learn to rise above it all. My concern is that we teach our children to be more compassionate and not always resort to violence in an unfortunate situation. The children today are so bright and full of energy. If we as parents teach them to positively channel that energy maybe they will be better, *less violent*, adults. I've gotten my daughters into swimming at the YWCA. They are both on the competitive swim team and compete for ribbons. I also seek out other after school activities to stimulate not only their bodies but their minds as well. I've enjoyed Kristen's enthusiasm this school year. Every day as soon as she gets in the car I hear 'Oooh Ma guess what." This shows me that she is enjoying what she's learning. I'd like to see her do better on her spelling and welcome any suggestions from both parents and you Mrs. Curry. I hope for an even more blessed year and want to say thanks.

Stephanie Rice

Keep up the excellent work!

Dear Ms. Rice,

I'm so glad that Kristen is having a good year for 6th grade. Like so many of her classmates she has jumped into all of her class work headfirst and she is doing very well.

What a wise mom you are! It is so good that you have your daughter in sports and other after school activities. I believe that these out of school experiences are just as necessary for developing well-rounded healthy young adults. Children can learn so much about making healthy, non-violent choices through these kinds of experiences. Especially for girls, sports helps them respect their bodies and themselves. There is a lot of new research about the

positive effect of organized sports activities for girls. Boys have always bene-
fited from sports experiences and now the girls are enjoying those benefits
too.

Thanks so much for your thoughtful journal response.

Sincerely,

Toby Curry

The Roving Parent Journal accomplishes much more than a simple and
direct dialogue between teacher and parent. Of course it takes time and attention, and for both teachers and parents the ensuing dialogue has to justify such
a commitment. Think about how the roving nature of the parent journal creates a community through writing and reading. The idea of parents and children keeping a journal together is also powerful, and it is obvious that excerpts
from the Roving Parent Journal are shared with the entire family when it
becomes that family's turn to enter into the dialogue. The ongoing nature of
this dialogue is what forms the learning com-
munity. At the same time, things are learned
from letter to letter—and learned not just at
school but at home. Each dialogue between
Toby and a family offers a window into the
classroom and into the home. Goals are set, concerns are raised. The past is
filled in, and the future contemplated. A definition of teacher is offered, and so
is one of learner. There's a plea to respect individual differences, a glimpse of a
class presentation on Japan, a play on conflict resolution, and expressions of
parents' recurring concern about the physical safety of their children. Although
Toby has never had a parent who did not themselves write, part of the opening
invitation from the teacher could mention the possibility of parents using their
children, family members, or friends as scribes to record their entries. If the
underlying purpose of the Roving Parent Journal is communication, whatever
helps make that communication happen needs to be encouraged.

In a presentation at the 1998 NCTE Conference in Albequerque, Toby
Curry outlined her

*"I am a single parent. My sons are
my life."*

Top Ten Reasons to Keep a Roving Parent Journal

10. Helps parents know what's going on in the classroom.
9. Ongoing way for the teacher to talk curriculum.
8. Keeps the parents connected to one another.
7. Builds a stronger classroom community.

6.   Models adult literacy for the kids.

5.   Models writing for the parents.

4.   Builds self-esteem for the children, the parents, and the teacher.

3.   Gives parents a chance to talk about parenting and schooling.

2.   Gives busy, overwhelmed parents a doorway into school. (Most middle school kids don't want their parents hanging around school very often.)

1.   It's a great teacher research project.

WHAT YOU CAN DO

Here is a brief guide to using the Roving Parent Journal.

First, some ideas on *getting started*:

- It helps if students are using journals in school and that they have some classroom experience with dialogue journals.
- Communicate with parents in advance about the journal:
  - Explain that it's a place for parents to raise questions or concerns about school.
  - Tell them it can be written by the parent or recorded by one of their children, or by a friend, relative, or other family member.
- Realize that the teacher's initial letter of communication with parents sets the tone. Toby Curry's initial communication is a handwritten "Dear Parents" letter.
- To initiate the journal, the teacher might choose to begin with a parent who would feel comfortable with setting sail first. "Whose mom or dad," Toby Curry asks her students, "really likes to write?"

Next, some ideas on *managing the journal*:

- Make certain the Roving Parent Journal is physically sturdy enough to travel and large enough not to get lost.
- Transport the Roving Parent Journal in a sturdy, identifiable (decorated?) envelope.
- Photocopy your response to the parent before sending the journal to another home. Send the photocopied response to the parent.
- Students are the couriers of the journal, so some discussion of that role and its responsibilities (prompt delivery) needs to take place in the classroom.

- Try to respond promptly. Toby recommends two entries a week, but knows that some weeks she will fall behind. "Then," she says, "I refer to it as my 'I'm Sorry Journal.'"
- Be realistic about how much time parents will need to write their response. It is important that the keeping of the journal not create stress for either parents or the teacher.
- The journal can also be a good place for the teacher to communicate information about classroom activities.

Finally, *follow up*:

- Because you photocopy your responses to parents before sending the journal to another family, you may continue a dialogue with individual parents who request additional information.
- Publish the entire journal for all parents at the end of the year. The roving nature of the journal creates a community of writers, but without end-of-year publication parents who participate early will miss out on most of the dialogue. Ask parents for help in assembling and distributing the publication. Then, celebrate publication with parents and students.

Chapter 7

Whose Standards Are They?

Milwaukee Metropolitan High School student Richard Gaines
reflects on the proposed Milwaukee Public High School
Admission Standards (from Rethinking Schools, Winter 1997–
1998, p. 28).

*P*arents are as confused about education "standards" as everyone else. There are national standards, professional teaching association standards, state standards, district standards, school standards. In Wisconsin, standards have been issued by the Milwaukee Public School District, by the governor, by the State Department of Public Instruction, by members of the state legislature, and by individual schools. "TEST RESULTS WILL NOT BE PRETTY, STATE WARNS" headlined a front-page report in the *Milwaukee Journal Sentinel* (October 25, 1997).

It's hard to be against "standards"; for most people the word itself indicates attainment and a certain level of excellence. But the fact is that other than having a familiarity with the term and some sense of the educational debate surrounding it, most parents have little idea of how certain standards influence classroom practice and what they can do to help their children attain these elusive standards. Parents and families have, in general, been left out of the formulation of standards. The language of standards—rubrics, assessment, proficiency—is not particularly parent friendly and distances many parents from participation in the ongoing standards dialogue and debate. In addition, few, if any, parents and community members have been genuinely involved in the formulation of education standards, which, according to news accounts, will transform the very nature of learning.

If the standards movement is as important as everyone says it is, then it is particularly important to include parents. This can be accomplished in a number of ways—from children and young adults demonstrating to their parents how they have achieved certain standards, to teachers sending home clear and easy-to-understand definitions of how standards inform their classroom instruction.

"If you want to communicate with parents you have to make it understandable to Joe Six-Pack. Who knows what 'rubric' means?"

Four basic questions quickly emerge when parents meet to learn about and discuss education standards:

1. What is my child supposed to be learning in school (or third grade or math or in sixth-grade biology)?
2. How can I help my child meet this standard?
3. How do I know if my child is meeting the standard?
4. How do I know if these standards are the best ones for my child?

Through a grant from the Cross City Campaign for Urban School Reform and the Annenberg Foundation, Jacqueline Ward and I gathered a group of Milwaukee parents together in order to formulate a way of making the complexity of standards more understandable while also providing a forum for parents to voice their points of view about standards. A mother of two children enrolled in the Milwaukee Public Schools, Jacqueline co-leads Parent Projects and has long been active in trying to turn up the volume of parent voice in district decision making.

FIRST SESSION

Welcome

The first session began with our distributing name tags and giving a brief description of the program goals. Participants then introduced themselves and noted the ages of their children and where they attended school. Journals were distributed.

Presentation

Participants were asked to write or draw in their journals whatever came to their mind when they heard the term "education standards." After about five minutes, individuals shared one thought or observation from their journal. Some responses:

- "Standards are a basic level of knowledge we want all students to reach. What I want to know is whether there are standards for teachers too."
- "I think it is something all parents need to know something about."
- "The grading system—like a measuring bar."
- "Goals for achievement. The basic requirement for getting passed to the next grade."
- "With Hmong people we do not understand what is meant by education standards."
- "Guideline for quality."
- "Something you should know."
- "Who makes up the standards?"
- "It's what is to be expected from a group of people. We need to know what is expected from everyone. Teachers, administration, students."
- "Standards? Who knows? I don't know."
- "My daughter's science teacher sent home a list of what they were going to learn at the beginning of the year. But I'm sure they're totally different for other teachers at the school."

- "When school starts they send all this paperwork home, but it doesn't express standards of education but standards of conduct—how you act, get expelled, and kicked out. The majority is conduct. Hardly ever do they send home information about what kids are supposed to know."
- "I know there are standards for 4th grade because when my daughter got to fifth grade two students were held back because of 4th grade testing. But we had no idea of what they were."
- "Teachers know the standards, but we don't get them. Standards are done by a few select people, and we have nothing to do with them."
- "If we have school standards, who enforces them?"
- "If we really want to know the standards, the parents need to get more involved in the school."
- "Is grade level standard? If you're at grade level, are you at standard?"
- "Are they published in different languages?"

Jacqueline and I distributed copies of the *Final Draft of the Milwaukee Public Schools K–12 Teaching and Learning Goals and Standards*, a hefty document of 75 pages. Jacqueline related what it was like to get a copy. "MPS standards," she said, "are locked up in a closet at Central Office." When she initially called Central Office to get a copy of the MPS standards, Jacqueline told us, "Nobody knew what they were, first of all. Finally I was connected to a woman who mailed me a copy. When I called to get additional copies, I was told that the woman who sent the first copy was on vacation. When I asked for an alternative person to speak to, no one knew a thing about the standards or where I could find them. So I decided to take a trip down to Central Office to pick up the copies myself. I went to the very same office of the woman who sent me the first copy. The person in the desk next to hers didn't know what the standards were, what they looked like, or where they were. I happened to look in a closet next to the office, and I said 'Oh, that looks like them' because it had a red cover on it. And the woman said, 'Oh, I'm so glad you knew it had a red cover because I didn't know what you were talking about.'" Jacqueline concluded, "I find it sad that the people in this office didn't know what the school district's standards were or where they were."

From Jacqueline's experience, at least one thing was clear: physical access to academic standards is a prerequisite to parent involvement with these standards.

All of us spent the next twenty minutes perusing the lengthy and complex Milwaukee Public Schools standards booklet. We asked parents to focus on one of their children and the grade-level standards for that child. After everyone had taken the time to get a sense of the document, we asked for responses and reactions. In the general discussion that followed, a number of issues quickly surfaced:

- *Equity*. Although there were computer standards, students and classrooms had uneven access to computers. Although there were multicultural standards, some of the history books were outdated and didn't reflect a multicultural approach.

- *Access*. A number of parents found the language of the standards confusing and vague. Some wanted to know whether the standards had been translated into Spanish and Hmong. "What," asked a parent, "is an 'expository text'?" Many of us found the language and form of presentation intimidating; we also struggled to figure out a fourth-grade math Sample Performance Assessment. "Am I just not smart enough to understand this?" asked one perplexed parent.

- *Accountability*. Who was responsible for the standards, and how would they be communicated to students and parents? If a student was below standard, how could teachers and parents work together to help him or her? How were teachers evaluated according to the standards?

- *Purpose*. The intended audience of the standards document was unclear. Were the standards written for teachers, or parents, or students?

Read-Aloud

Because it refocused the discussion on individual students and the difficulty of measuring learning through STANDARDized tests, *First Grade Takes a Test*, written by Miriam Cohen and illustrated by Lillian Hoban, was a good choice as our read-aloud book. This picture book relates how an enthusiastic firstgrade class responded to their first standardized test. George wrote in an answer not included in a multiple-choice question about rabbits' eating preferences; Sammy got stuck on the question "What do firemen do?" because the multiple choices didn't include the time firemen got his uncle's head out of a "big pipe"; Jim was distracted by one of the test's illustrations. The only first grader to finish the test in the allotted time was Ann Maria. The test results propelled Ann Maria into a "special class" while her classmates began calling each other and themselves "dummy." The teacher interrupted the anger and self-loathing by explaining that the test "doesn't tell all the things you *can* do." The students then went on to demonstrate how much they actually knew in a brief yet compelling depiction of student-initiated inquiry and problem solving. Ann Maria's eventual desire to return to the rest of her first-grade classmates made the point that some things are more important than achieving the best test score. *First Grade Takes a Test* raised a number of issues related to standards—for example, were some ways of measuring student learning better than others?

At Home Activity

"Help me to make my child the best he can be. What does it take from me to change his C to a B?"

The parents decided that during the coming week they wanted to talk to their children about whether they were aware of classroom learning goals, and some parents intended to set up an appointment with their children's teachers in order to better understand how standards were affecting classroom instruction. We decided to invite a representative of the Milwaukee schools to speak to us about the district's standards and how parents could help their children achieve these standards.

FOLLOW-UP WORKSHOP: WHAT MAKES A COOKIE GOOD?

One of the most difficult things to understand is that what the standard is and how it is to be measured affects classroom teaching and learning. There is increasingly acrimonious debate about these issues, but until one has some firsthand experience with what it means to set a standard, implications of the debate are difficult to see clearly. In order to help participants gain experience in setting a standard, Jacqueline and I decided to conduct a "What Makes a Cookie Good?" workshop. (This workshop was modeled after a demonstration by Steven Zemelman at the Walloon Institute, Summer 1996.)

We began by passing out paper plates. Each participant was given three different kinds of cookies: a chocolate chip cookie, a low-calorie Fig Newton, and a sugar wafer. We formed into small groups to decide a question fortunes have been made and lost over: What makes a cookie good? How do we judge if we want to eat a second cookie or leave it alone? Each small group was to decide their cookie "standard" by group consensus and then rank the three cookies as to whether they were (1) above standard, (2) at standard, or (3) below standard. Groups were also to decide the form their final judgment would take: a letter grade, a number based on a point system, a narrative, or something else. Cookie packages were available if groups wanted to consult the list of ingredients or the nutritional/calorie information.

What followed was hilarious and informative, if not exactly nutritious. Those who were passionate about chocolate argued with those who were allergic. Some had strong memories associated with their favorite Fig Newtons; others would settle for nothing less than a fudge brownie, which was not even on our plates. And what was our criteria for judging what makes a cookie good? The group I was in finally settled on taste, appearance, nutrition, size, and cost—with the elusive and much-debated standard of taste counting double. Other groups had different standards, such as smell. Groups also had different ways of reporting their standards.

As we discussed the results, the implications of setting a standard were made clear. No matter how inviting a cookie's aroma, if smell was not a standard, it wouldn't be encouraged. In other words, how academic standards are defined determines what is taught, and therefore learned, in the classroom.

OTHER READ-ALOUDS

A provocative conclusion to the "What Makes a Cookie Good?" workshop was a read-aloud of *Through the Cracks* by Carolyn Sollman, Barbara Emmons, and Judith Paolini. As the title implies, *Through the Cracks* tells the story of students who have not only figuratively but literally failed to be supported by the educational system. In the world of this picture book there is an actual subterranean environment populated by children (and a teacher) who have literally fallen through schoolroom floors. The book has a lot to say about how classrooms can be organized and teaching transformed to regain those who have "fallen through the cracks."

A tour de force read-aloud guaranteed to leave readers and listeners breathless is *Math Curse* by Jon Scieszka (illustrated by Lane Smith). A mathematical progression of surreal and everyday details, *Math Curse* turns everyday activities into obsessive math problems yielding surprising and comic results. *Math Curse* expresses one of the best principles of the standards movement: the practical demonstration of learning in everyday experience.

And what about standards for teachers? Billy of *Billy and the Bad Teacher* by Andrew Clements (illustrated by Elivia Savadier) has very strict standards for his teacher, Mr. Adams. Billy intends to communicate his standards to the principal, the mayor, the governor, and the president of the United States.

A classic picture book that has gained new meaning in light of the standards movement is *Leo the Late Bloomer* by Robert Kraus, illustrated by José Aruego, in which Leo reminds us that standards must not be so restrictive that there is no room for everyone to finally bloom.

WHAT OTHERS ARE DOING

Ruth Mitchell of The Education Trust in Washington, D.C., has developed an approach for working with teachers and classroom standards that also works well with parents. The process involves participants in actually doing a performance assessment and generating a scoring guide based on the classroom standards and an assignment question. Using the scoring guide, participants score actual student responses to the same assessment. The crucial part of the process is for participants to ask two questions: (1) Does the student's work meet the standard? (2) If it does not, what can we do about it? Ruth asks, "What action can we plan at the classroom, school, district, state levels, so that all students meet the standard? . . . What can we as individual(s) . . . do tomorrow to improve student learning?"

Many teachers involve students in the communication of classroom learning standards to their parents by arranging student-led parent conferences. In these conferences, students talk directly to their parents about their academic progress, demonstrating what they have achieved through specific reference to work in their portfolios; and together they set goals (standards) for the next grading period. Student-led parent conferences not only clarify what standards mean in terms of academic performance for both parents and students, they also encourage student reflection, ownership of learning, and sense of responsibility. For further information regarding student-led parent conferences see *Changing the View: Student-Led Parent Conferences* by Terri Austin (1994).

WHAT YOU CAN DO

Don't keep your classroom learning goals a secret from students or parents. Verbally and in writing frequently communicate your learning goals to parents and display them prominently in your classroom. Make sure your classroom goals are written in a language accessible to parents and their children (avoid academic jargon). Use your students to help communicate these goals by arranging frequent opportunities for parents to experience and enjoy their children's academic performance.

Invite parents of your students to a meeting to discuss how they can help their children achieve academic success. In these meetings, give specific examples of what parents can do at home to help their children achieve classroom learning goals. Show parents how your classroom goals support lifelong learning. One way to do this is to invite parents to reflect on their dreams for their children's future. In a Chicago Parent Project on standards, Pete Leki asked parents to create an idea web with one of their children at the center.

My dream and wish to my God is this. I dream that the Lord let me live to see all three of my children grown up to be fine young men and ladies. That they finish eighth grade and four years of high school. It's up to them if they want to go to college. Jasmine dreams to go into the Navy. Jason would like to be a policeman or sing or dance. Well Denise is a whole new show. Denise don't know what she wants to be. Whatever they decide is alright with me because they are the one who have to deal with their self. Only thing I teach my children. Learn to love your self and respect your self. The rest will fall in place.

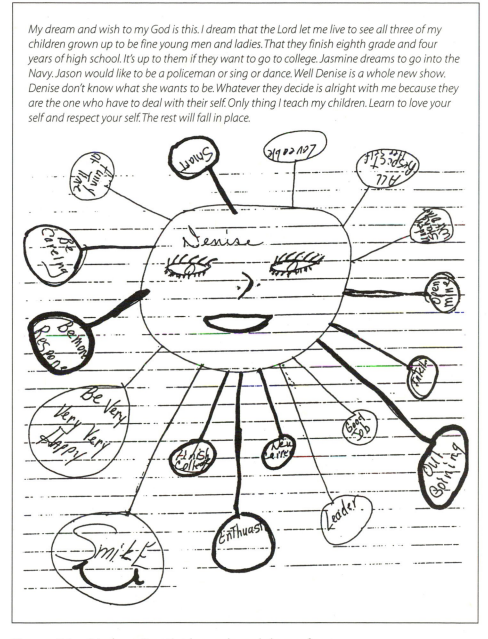

Figure 7.1   Marlene Scott's idea web and dream for her children.

He invited parents to imagine their child as an adult at some point in the future. "How do you want your child to turn out? What are your dreams for that child?" he asked. Parents shared their dreams and then considered how their school could help their child become that kind of adult. (See Figure 7.1 for an example.) How do classroom goals fit into parents' dreams, thus making them more possible?

Chapter 8

The Legend of the Bright Blue Bush

Welcoming parents by providing a comfortable, spacious meeting place, Stockton School, Chicago.

*T*he Legend of the Bright Blue Bush goes like this: "One cold winter day I was driving past the school, and there was this bright blue bush near the entrance. It was almost surreal—everything else was kind of drab in contrast to the bright color. I stopped the car and got out to see what it was. The bush was plastered with bright blue paper. This was where the students threw away the notes to parents on their way home from school."

Perhaps it is time to reconsider how schools communicate to parents and change some prevalent attitudes toward family involvement in schools. A news report on reading test scores in the *Milwaukee Journal Sentinel* (December 29, 1997) focused on a Milwaukee elementary school that had the lowest reading scores in the state. A factor mentioned as contributing to these scores was the low parent involvement. When interviewed by the newspaper's reporter, the school's reading specialist said that in order to increase parent involvement he had invited school parents to a meeting on a weekday morning. "About a half dozen parents attended; they were outnumbered by school staff members," he complained (p. 6A). The net effect of the *Journal Sentinel* article was to portray parents as uninterested in their children's learning and blame them for their children's low test scores. Apparently no one thought that a weekday morning might not be the most convenient time to hold a parents' meeting.

A few months earlier, the Milwaukee Public School Board's Innovation and School Reform Committee had met to consider a plan to give parents and community members a greater role in governing schools. In a letter opposing the plan, the staff of Eighth Street School told the school board that "some parents are known to have an adverse effect upon the care, development and education of their children. . . . In some instances, parents are known to be the cause of their children's school problems" (*Milwaukee Journal Sentinel*, October 8, 1997, p. 1A). One parent in the audience responded that parents are often encouraged to become involved in schools, only to be "treated as a nuisance" when they try. "You need to act like we're welcome," she said (p. 6).

"I went to parent-teacher conferences. It was in a big gym and parents signed up. Then we sat in the gym lined up in chairs like we were in time out. It was the last time I'll go to a conference like that."

What, then, does it mean to "welcome" parents into schools? First of all, it means using innovative ways of communicating with parents—especially if you notice the equivalent of a bright blue bush adjacent to the school property. Welcoming parents also means viewing them as allies in their children's education, not as obstacles to that education. The lack of a parent's physical presence at school does not necessarily mean a lack of motivation or interest. Blaming parents for a perceived lack of involvement will not miraculously produce the desired involvement; urging parent involvement only to treat them with disdain discourages the kind of partnerships necessary for children's educational success. In most instances, the parent connection is the primary factor in learning.

Our work with parents has convinced us that welcoming parents means that we:

- Assume that parents want their children to succeed in school and want to help their children succeed.

- Understand that many parents have been excluded from the dialogue surrounding education and are unclear about school terminology and how they can support classroom instruction.

- Begin with a group of parents (no matter how small) and work with them to devise a plan for increasing parent involvement.

- Consider whether the school really wants parent involvement or is merely espousing the term for political expedience. Is there, for example, a parent room or center, facilities for child care, some basic amenities (like coffee), a way of dealing with language differences?

- Understand that a parent's time is of equal value to a teacher's time. Perhaps a parent meeting at 9:00 A.M. is convenient for teachers, but not at all convenient for parents. In other words, is there any accommodation for parents' schedules?

- Do not necessarily assume that parents don't care simply because they are not present at school. There are many ways for parents to become involved in their children's education, and it is what parents do to encourage learning in the home that is most crucial.

AN ATTITUDE ADJUSTMENT WORKSHOP

Welcome

Bama Grice is a Milwaukee parent with a son in the sixth grade. She works full time and also attends school at night in pursuit of a college degree. Bama has been active in parent organizing, and she has a business card with ATTITUDE ADJUSTMENT CONSULTANT printed in the center. Bama asked each of the teachers and parents in her workshop to introduce themselves to the rest of the group: name, school, or grade level of children. She asked us, "What do you think of when you hear the words 'attitude adjustment'?"

Read-Aloud

For the read-aloud we listened to *Willy the Wimp* by Anthony Browne. Poor Willy, the scrawny gorilla, was treated like a wimp until he sent away for some mail-order fitness programs that turned him into a muscular hunk—or at least that was how he started to view himself. Then came the cold reality, which literally hit him in the face as he walked into a pole and deflated back into being a wimp. *Willy the Wimp* was not only an entertaining and surprising read-aloud, it also adjusted everyone's attitude a little about the sophisticated level of many children's books. *Willy the Wimp* started all of us thinking about how important yet elusive "attitude" is.

Workshop

Bama asked us what we do when we want to invite friends over to our home. Did we make a special call? Did we send out a nice invitation? Did we make plans to clean our house? Bama then asked, "What do schools do when they want parents to come in? Send home a flier mixed up with the children's homework? Pin a note to a mitten?"

"What we are talking about," said Bama, "is an attitude adjustment."

Bama had each of us choose an index card. There were four different colored cards to choose from. Once everyone held their card, we were grouped according to our color preference. The members of the four groups were given fifteen minutes to reach consensus about what they would like to see happen in terms of parent-teacher collaboration in schools.

Each group chose a member to speak for the group, and Bama listed the points each group had come up with on a large chart. After some discussion, Bama asked each of us to decide on one thing we could do to improve the relationship between parents and teachers, family and school. "Choose something that can be done," she told us. "If there's nothing you think you can do, then we need to talk about it."

Later, I asked Bama what had made her become a parent advocate. "MPS [the Milwaukee Public Schools] robbed me of my education," she said. "I won't let the same thing happen to another child."

WHAT OTHERS ARE DOING

Enthusiasm for their children's learning motivates most parents, and displays of this learning always provide a good opportunity to strengthen the family-school connection. In a recent issue of *Rethinking Schools* (1998) fifth-grade teacher Bob Peterson describes an "exhibition" that culminates the academic career of students at La Escuela Fratney, a kindergarten-through-fifth-grade Milwaukee public school. The exhibition of student projects—from historical research, to poster-size surveys of classmates, to stories and essays—encourages students to reflect on and demonstrate what they have learned during their five years at Fratney. Each student's exhibit contains an autobiography, a self-portrait, a name poem, a time line, a description of numbers in the student's life, and a "postcard" for each year—"on one side drawing a picture of a memorable event and on the other writing about it as they would have at the time" (p. 15). The goal of the exhibition, writes Peterson, is "to increase students' intrinsic motivation to do quality work." The audience for the exhibition is the entire school community—teachers, students, and parents. "Parents are definitely pleased to see what their kids have accomplished. One comment we often hear is 'I wish I would have gone to a fifth grade where I did projects like this'" (p. 15).

In a study prepared for the Council of Chief State School Officers, researcher Reginald Clark points out that the effectiveness of parent outreach is directly related to the quality of the school's educational program. As reported in *CATALYST—Voices of Chicago School Reform*, Clark notes, "Poorly organized school programs are not in the best position to effectively cultivate parent and community support" (1990, p. 2). He recommends six steps for parent involvement (p. 2):

1. Develop stimulating curricular offerings . . . and active teaching.
2. Assess current state of home-school relations.
3. Create an inviting climate.
4. Catalogue available resources.
5. Find ways to put parents in face-to-face communication with friendly and supportive school staff.
6. Write a plan for parent involvement activities in support of all curricular areas.

WHAT YOU CAN DO

Remember the Legend of the Bright Blue Bush. If your means of communicating with parents isn't working, try something else. Be persistent and rely on numerous ways of staying in touch with parents. Set up telephone trees, newsletters, and opportunities for dialogue with family members (both written and oral). Provide a place for parent response on grade reports, at the end of books published by children, and as a "clip and return" section of the classroom or school newsletter. Communicate good news to parents about the school, your class, and their children's learning.

Perhaps the crucial attitude adjustment has to do with our sense of the possibilities for family involvement. What we think is possible often determines what happens.

Now is an opportune time to look in detail at the Family History Parent Project—a project that really hits home.

Chapter 9

Family History: The Project that Hits Home

Family quilt square, Family History Parent Project,
Allen Field School, Milwaukee.

*T*here are times when parents and family do not just support the classroom curriculum, but move to the center of the curriculum. Such was the case with the Family History Project for seventh- and eighth-grade students at Jenner School, located in Chicago's Cabrini-Green public housing complex. The Family History curriculum was developed by Pat Bearden and Yolanda Simmons, sisters and former Chicago public school teachers currently on the faculty of National-Louis University's Center for City Schools. Because they are sisters, Pat and Yolanda's interest in family history was personal as well as professional, and the curriculum was designed to teach critical thinking, history, multicultural awareness, and inquiry through a concentration on family and community history. For Jenner students this meant a four-month sequence of classroom activities that were designed to be alive, breathing with historical memories and records. It was a curriculum not only enhanced but dependent on parent participation and understanding. "Family History," as Pat and Yolanda enthusiastically defined it, was "the curriculum that hits home!"

In a letter sent to Jenner parents, Pat and Jenner principal Sandy Satinover described the classroom focus on family history as a way for students to develop "better critical thinking skills and a greater sense of family heritage, community, and global history." Parents were also invited to participate in a parallel Family History Parent Project, which would consist of six two-hour weekly workshops to be conducted by Pat and Pete Leki.

FIRST SESSION

Welcome
Paired interviews
Presentation about family history
Read-aloud: On the Day You Were Born *by Debra Frasier*
At Home journal activity: the day one of your children was born

Pat and Pete handed out name tags, pens, and journals; introduced themselves; and gave a brief description of the Project goals, the weekly meeting times, the stipends, child care arrangements, and other organizational details.

Participants were to use journals to jot down notes from the paired interviews. In the interviews, parents asked and responded to the same questions that their children used in their respective classrooms:

1. What is your ethnic makeup?
2. When did your people first come to Chicago?
3. Who were the first family members to come to Chicago?

4. Where did they come from (state, city, and/or country outside the United States)?
5. Why did they come to Chicago?
6. What types of jobs did they get when they arrived?
7. What jobs did they have before they came to Chicago?
8. In which wars have your relatives served?

After the interviews, each person introduced his or her partner to the whole group, using family history details in the introduction. Pete and Pat noted on chart paper the participants' ethnic backgrounds, places of origin, and dates of migration to Chicago. The resulting classroom profile was, Pete and Pat pointed out, the beginning of a data base describing the historical context of this particular learning community.

Ethnic Background

Italian, Black

Cherokee

Creole, White, Chinese

Puerto Rico

Polish, Gypsy, African

Barbadian

Dutch

Gigie

Where From	Moved To	
	Chicago	*Cabrini*
Port Gibson, Mississippi	1959	1975
Bayfield, Mississippi	1955	1993
Jackson, Mississippi		1965
Swiftown, Mississippi	1947	1961
Chicago, Illinois		1965
Chicago, Illinois		1980
Chicago, Illinois		1988

(continued)

Where From	Moved To	
	Chicago	*Cabrini*
Chicago, Illinois		1978
Helena, Arkansas	1988	1988
Natchez, Mississippi		1977
Blyville, Arkansas		1950/70
Greenville, Mississippi	1950	1960s
Airville, South Carolina	1952	
Lambert, Mississippi	1963	1963
Memphis, Tennessee	1950	1968
Oceola, Arkansas	1934	1973

After a break filled with good food, drinks, and conversation, Pat helped the group brainstorm where they could find more information about their own family history. The many suggestions included family photo albums, interviews with relatives, the Chicago Public Library (and other local libraries), old letters, the Bible, artifacts, music, old neighbors, the Illinois Historical Society, high school yearbooks, videotapes, even family recipes.

A read-aloud of Debra Frasier's picture book *On the Day You Were Born* concluded this initial Family History workshop on a note of new beginnings and fond remembrance. Through Frasier's paper collage illustrations, the moon, tides, animals, and other forces of nature rejoice in the day each person was born.

The At Home journal activity during the coming week was suggested by the read-aloud: either through drawing or writing, parents were invited to reflect on the day one of their children was born.

SECOND SESSION
Welcome
Journal sharing: the day your child was born
Family tree workshop
Journal activity: a relative from your family tree
Read-aloud: "The Feeling That You Have" from The Wiz
At Home: Continue family tree; share character sketch of a relative with your
*   family; and, if possible, find a photograph of that relative*

Even if parents didn't complete the journal writing about the day their child was born, Pat and Pete encouraged everyone to share something at the start of the second session—a remembrance or something that happened during the week.

As Pete played a Curtis Mayfield CD, Pat commented on how music can be a communal source of joy and pride, reaffirming the larger historic context of the Cabrini-Green community. In addition to Curtis Mayfield, other musicians from the community included Jerry Butler, the Impressions, and Major Lance.

The sharing of "The Day Your Child Was Born" journal entries connected everyone emotionally to the family history inquiry at hand. Parent Carolyn Lee wrote about her daughter:

Loretta

Loretta was born in Chicago on November 29, 1989. I loved her the first day she was born. I had a hard time delivering her, because she acted like she did not want to come out. It was like she wanted to stay in side of me forever. They finally had to take her, but I was to see her beautiful face anyway.

Pat demonstrated how to fill out a family tree by using her own family history and displaying it on an overhead projector (see the family tree templates in Appendix C). Pat's encouragement for everyone to remember distant family members' names started people thinking about how they could research their homes for documents, photographs, and other reminders.

As part of the family tree workshop, Pat asked everyone to concentrate on one individual from their family tree. "Try to picture that person, remember him or her. Focus on things said or specific things that happened. If a photograph is available, look it over and consider the parts—clothes, background, hairstyle, eyes, mouth, characteristic expression. . . . Try to work with the details. Write a few sentences describing the person through some detail about him or her. Try to tell some memory or detail that will make this person stand out as a real individual." After people had finished their reflections, they shared what they had written in small groups. Through the writing and sharing of these sketches, the family trees began to come to life.

Written by Charlie Smalls, "The Feeling That We Have" (from the 1978 musical *The Wiz*) is a song about treasuring the love between parent and child through the vagaries of time. The song's refrain, "Don't lose the feeling that we had," seemed to sum up the embrace of family and history at the center of the workshop sessions.

Pete and Pat asked parents and teachers to continue their research at home during the week between sessions in order to fill in more of the blank spaces on their family tree. Research might be in the home, throughout the extended family, or in archives and libraries. Parents were also encouraged to share the biographical sketch about a relative with the rest of their family. Pat suggested that individuals try to find a picture of the relative they wrote about to bring to the next session. "Call them up if they are alive. Or call someone close to them who can remind you of more things about them and their life." The sketch of a relative was certain to stir other memories and elicit more inquiry.

THIRD SESSION

Welcome
Sharing of something from your family history ·
Family history time line workshop
Read-aloud: "Death Corner"
At Home: Time lines of our children's lives
Reflection: How are we doing?

The welcome at the start of the third session involved not only filling out name tags, but also giving help with family trees and/or journal writing, bringing in music from the community, and sharing classroom library books.

Pete and Pat asked everyone to introduce themselves by sharing something from their family history: a journal entry, their family tree, a family artifact, documents, photos, or some family news. Participants read about great-grandmothers, nieces, cousins, parents, grandparents, even a beloved dog. As parents read their character sketches, a sense of community history also began to emerge. Rodger Hemphill's sketch was memorable:

Ms. Carrie Ann Cade

Born on April 15, 1900 in Airville, South Carolina. She was the daughter of the late Perry and Lizzie Hopper.

She departed this life Saturday, November 13, 1993 at Chicago Osteopathic Hospital in Chicago, Ill.

She leaves to mourn 15 nieces and nephews, a host of great nieces and nephews and many, many friends.

Her favorite song was "Walk With Me Lord." She was a very sweet and loving person and put her heart out to everyone.

When Carrie moved to Chicago she stayed at 660 W. Division. Which is located between Halsted and Larrabee. She stayed on the 6th floor. Then she went back home to Airville, South Carolina, and stayed for ten years. She moved back to Chicago in the 60's in the same building but on the 7th floor this time.

Back in those days there were deliverymen that came through the neighborhood every other Saturday morning delivering eggs, milk, orange and fruit juice.

The Cabrini Green residents were more safer and what I mean about safer is children, mother, father, and friend got along very much better then family's do today.

Pat began the time line workshop by having everyone brainstorm their own individual time lines. "How far back do they go?" "What are some of the *big* dates?" "How do we chart them out?" "How does this relate to math?" Parents enthusiastically went about the construction of their time lines in individual and informative ways. Many of the notations were like chapter synopses—windows onto a biographical landscape ever present with additional family history and personal narrative (see Figures 9.1 and 9.2).

After giving participants time to work and share, Pat extended the process to include family time lines and community time lines. These were, she said, ongoing, long-term projects. She asked, "Can we combine all three time lines—individual, family, and community? How does this relate to the study of history and social studies?"

The read-aloud, "Death Corner," was a newspaper excerpt from the 1920s describing the then-Sicilian neighborhood at Cabrini. "Death Corner" got participants thinking about ways the neighborhood had changed and what had stayed the same.

During the next week, everyone was encouraged to make time lines of their children's lives, being sure to include events that were important to the children. Pat encouraged parents to overlap their time line with their children's and think about the similarities and differences.

The session ended with a brief reality check. "How are we doing?" Pete asked. "If you need extra help, try to come fifteen minutes early next week."

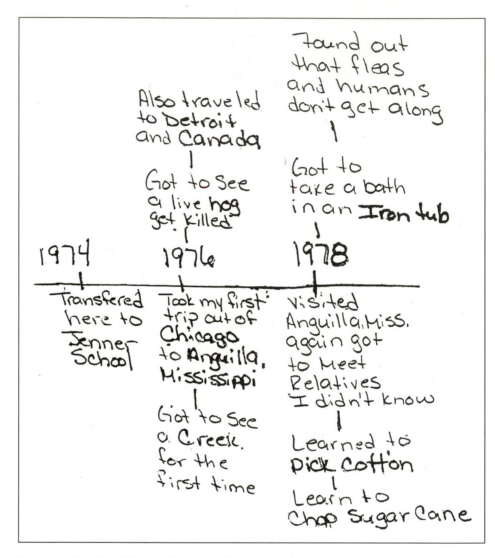

Figure 9.1   Detail from Gloria Davis's personal history
time line.

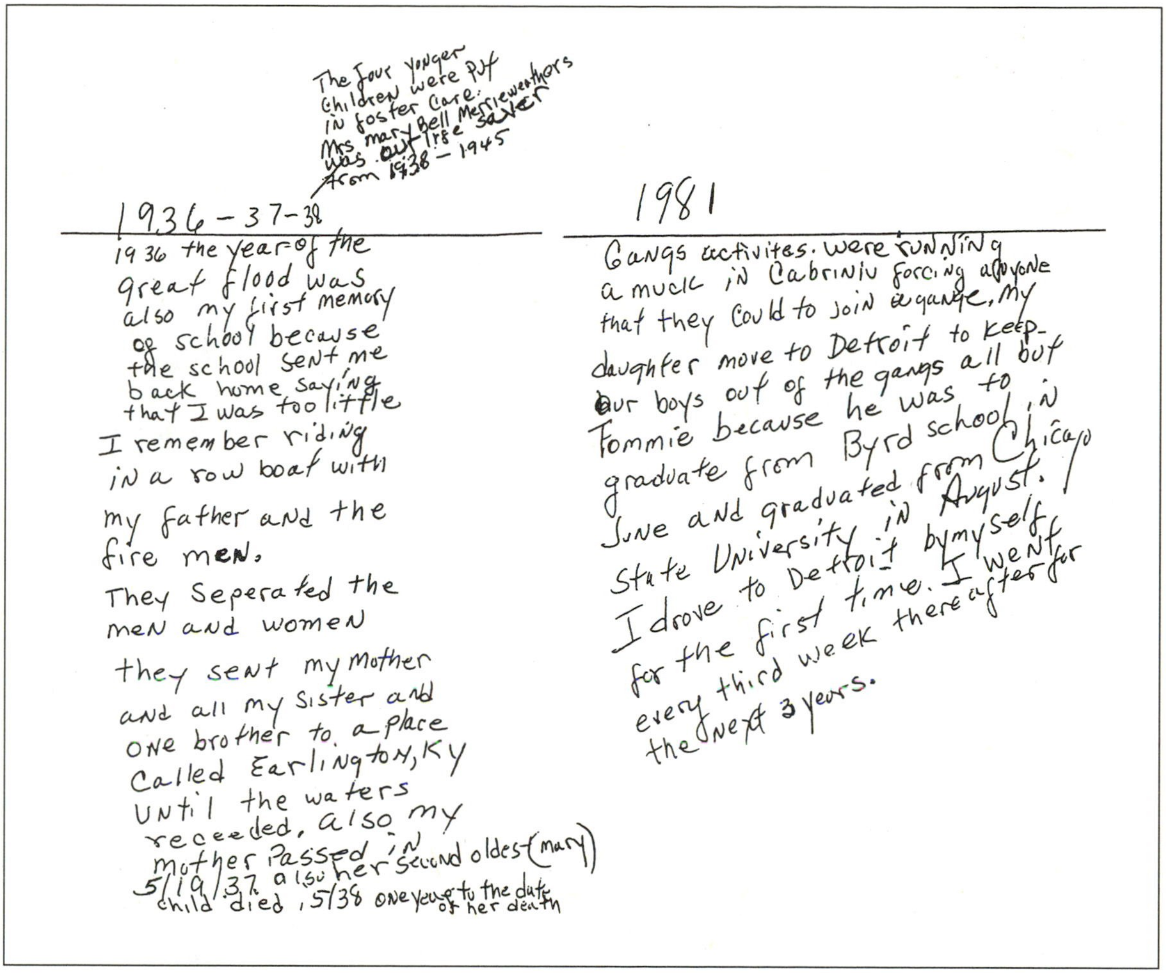

The four younger
children were put
in foster care.
Mrs. Mary Bell Merrieweathers
was our Irse saver
from 1938 - 1945

1936 - 37 - 38

1936 the year of the
great flood was
also my first memory
of school because
the school sent me
back home saying
that I was too little

I remember riding
in a row boat with

my father and the
fire men.

They seperated the
men and women

they sent my mother
and all my sister and
one brother to a place
called Earlington, KY
until the waters
receeded, also my
mother passed in
5/19/37, also her second oldest (mary)
child died, 5/38 one year to the date
of her death

1981

Gangs activites. were running
a muck in Cabrinin forcing anyone
that they could to join a gange. My
daughter move to Detroit to keep
our boys out of the gangs all but
Tommie because he was to
graduate from Byrd school in
June and graduated from Chicago
State University in August.
I drove to Detroit bymyself
for the first time. I went
every third week thereafter for
the next 3 years.

Figure 9.2   Two details from Cozella Brown's
twelve-foot-long personal history time line.

FOURTH SESSION
Welcome
Sharing: Something from your family history
Read-aloud: Brown Angels *by Walter Dean Meyers*
Neighborhood workshop
At Home: Document a favorite neighborhood place with your children
Reflection: How's it going?

Many parents arrived at the fourth session early to select and return books, listen to music from the community, make copies of documents from their at-home research, and get help with the construction of their family trees and time lines.

As participants assembled, they shared something from their family history research: their time line, their children's time lines, new information from their family tree. Comments about good books or other news was also welcomed. Everyone was eager to see each other's time lines as well as how they related to those done by the children. (An example of one of the children's time lines is given in Figure 9.3).

Using an overhead projector, Pat presented various types of time lines and demonstrated different ways of recording important moments—births, deaths, marriage—as well as comic and tragic incidents. Pat talked about how time line notations can be the genesis of stories that further illuminate family history. She showed how personal time lines can be overlaid with historical time lines, thus putting personal lives in a historical perspective.

Since many parents and teachers brought in old photographs of relatives, Walter Dean Meyers' *Brown Angels* served as an inspiring read-aloud. *Brown Angels* documents and celebrates African American childhood through authentic turn-of-the-century photographs and expressive poems.

Family history is closely connected to community history, so Pat and Pete distributed enlarged local street maps of the Cabrini neighborhood and asked parents to work in small groups to identify and label places of interest: Jenner School, their homes, Seward Park, various streets, and so forth.

After fifteen minutes, Pat reassembled the group and, returning to the overhead projector, constructed a composite neighborhood map. The At Home activity would involve everyone in a further exploration of the Cabrini neighborhood. Parents were given index cards and single-use cameras and asked to document, sometime during the week, a favorite neighborhood place with

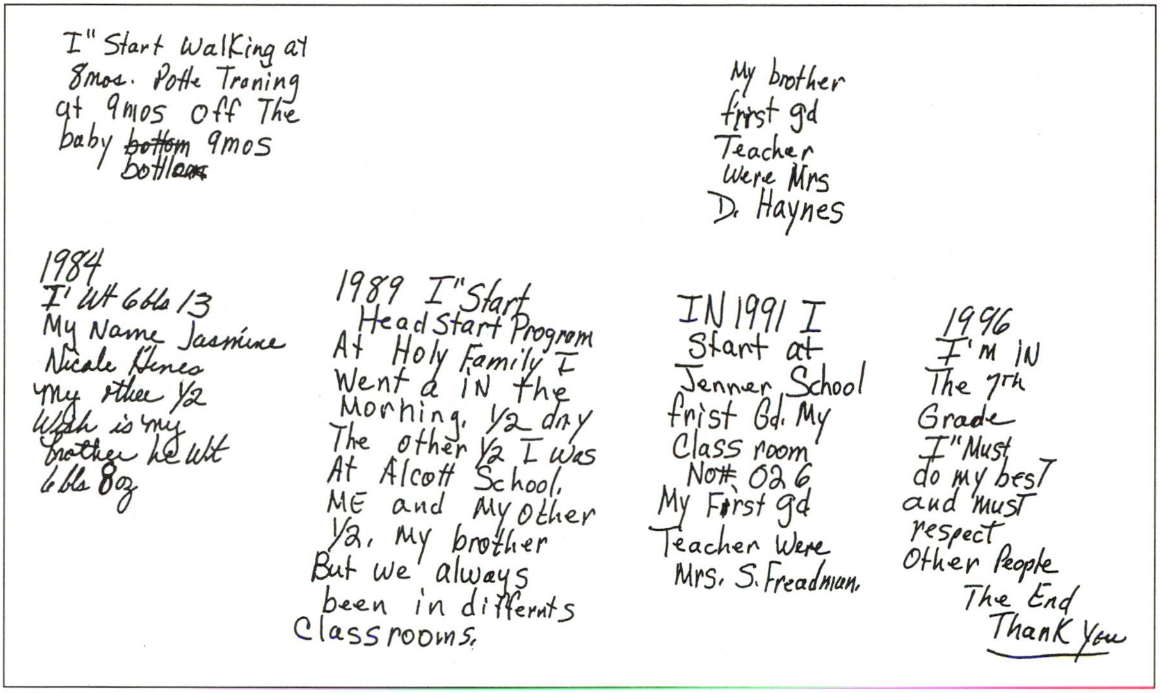

I" Start walking at
8mos. Potte Troning
at 9mos off The
baby ~~bottom~~ 9mos
bottlem

My brother
frrst gd
Teacher
Were Mrs
D. Haynes

1984
I' Wt 6lb 13
My Name Jasmine
Nicole Hines
my other 1/2
Wish is my
brother he Wt
6lb 8oz

1989 I" Start
Head Start Program
At Holy Family I
Went a IN the
Morning, 1/2 day
The other 1/2 I was
At Alcott School,
ME and My other
1/2, my brother
But we always
been in differnts
Classrooms,

IN 1991 I
Start at
Jenner School
frist Gd. My
Class room
No# 026
My First gd
Teacher Were
Mrs, S. Freadman,

1996
I'M IN
The 7th
Grade
I" Must
do my best
and must
respect
Other People
The End
Thank You

Figure 9.3   Personal time line of Jasmine Nicole Hines
(daughter of Marlene Scott).

their children. "Working with your children," she said, "photograph a neighborhood place that has special significance—a place that holds strong memories and associations. On the index card, describe what your photo shows. Where is it? What happened there? What memories are attached to the place? What used to be there a long time ago? What is going to happen to this place? These stories about memorable places will combine to tell a history of the neighborhood called Cabrini-Green."

Once again, before people left the workshop, Pat and Pete asked for reflection and comments: "Questions?" "How are we doing?" And, echoing the last line from "The Feeling That You Have," Pat bid good-bye with "Don't lose that feeling that we have."

FIFTH SESSION
Welcome
Sharing and neighborhood map work
Read-aloud: Everybody Needs a Rock by Byrd Baylor
At Home: Find your own rock, locate it on the neighborhood map, and describe the
*   rock in your journal*
Reflection

For the fifth session, many Family History Parent Project participants again arrived early to check out or return resources, get help with their family trees and time lines, have family and community historical documents photocopied, and listen to music from the community.

As people introduced themselves, there was a large selection of family history artifacts from which to share, and parents and teachers needed to limit their choices. Pat and Pete had tape recorders available for people who hadn't written anything and wanted to record oral history. Pete recorded Mary Dawson's "Remembering Too-loo":

Daddy had just come from the spillway on the river. That's the only time I remember him working. 'Cause he was a hunter in that place where we used to live.

My sisters wanted to go to the movies. They wanted to see that big . . . gorilla . . . King Kong. They asked me to watch the baby. I was 18 or 19. My momma said, "Get your brother's pants. I wanna put a patch on 'em." She said, "That baby gonna give you trouble. You'd do anything to make some money."

All of a sudden she slump. She said, "Get me some water."

I went to the kitchen and got some water. But she couldn't even drink. The water just slide right out the side of her mouth.

I started hollering like a crazy person. Ms. Sawzee hear me. She was a gospel singer—like Mahalia Jackson—at our church.

She says, "What's wrong?"

I say, "My mother dead."

"Naw. Too-loo ain't dead."

"Yes, she dead. She dead."

Ms. Sawzee, she brought a mirror and held it up to her. And then she know she was dead.

She told me go get my sisters.

I ran to that movie theater. I don't know what happen to the baby. I got there and run in. The lady stop me, says you can't go in there without paying. I say, "I have to find my sister. My momma dead."

"No. . . ."

"Yes, she dead. When they left she was alive and now she dead. Can you make an announcement."

So they call out in the theater if the Andrews sisters were there. And then we went home and someone had called the undertaker.

We was well known in New Orleans in our neighborhood. We didn't have no money. But people knew about the Andrews.

As the single-use cameras were collected (in order to arrange for the film to be developed), parents described the location of their special neighborhood place and read notes from their index cards. Once developed, the photographs would be put with the index cards, to serve as another visual juncture of personal and community history. As parents described the location of their special neighborhood places, Pat and Pete located and marked the individual sites on the Cabrini neighborhood map.

Everybody Needs a Rock by Byrd Baylor, with pictures by Peter Parnall, is a book about cherishing the small pieces of homeland. It gives ten fanciful, yet practical, rules for finding that special rock. The At Home activity for the week was for parents and children to search for such a unique rock in the Cabrini neighborhood. "Tell us where the rock was found. Locate the site on your neighborhood map. Describe the rock in the journal." The rock activity tied into the photographs of special neighborhood places. "What," Pat asked, "does the type of rock tell us about the history of this place called Cabrini-Green?"

During the coming week, parents and teachers were to look through their portfolio of time lines, artifacts, documents, reflections, and sketches and choose one item to be included in the Family History parent publication. Pat and Pete generated the portfolio list of possibilities for publication:

Life time line

Stories about relatives

Family history documents

Photographs (the older the better! Label, date, and photocopy)

Genealogical tree

Photographs of the neighborhood with written descriptions

Rocks—a rock found in the neighborhood—describe it and its history

Journal entries

FINAL SESSION
Welcome and display of rocks
Return of developed photographs of special neighborhood places
Sharing of writing for family history publication
Family tree workshop
Evaluation
Celebration

When parents and teachers brought their found rocks to the final workshop session, they found an empty shelf on which they could display their rocks along with their respective journal reflections.

Developed photographs of special places in the neighborhood were returned. The photographs created a lot of interest and caused everyone to look at the Cabrini neighborhood map with a new sense of specificity. There were photographs of small residential gardens, previous residences, a playground, janitors shoveling snow from in front of the school, a vacant lot "where I used to live." Mrs. Ferris's photograph of the vacant lot also showed her daughter holding up Mrs. Ferris's pet dog, Princess (aka Pride and Joy). Below the photograph, Mrs. Ferris wrote:

> This picture is about where I used to live, me and my mother and sisters but the building was knocked down. It was 1119 N. Cleveland.
> I got off from work an one of my twins had my dog, Princess, walking her.
> I love my Pride and Joy.
> She gave my life, nobody but not never hurt her.
> I will fight for her.

The emotion Mrs. Ferris brought to the photograph of her dog was especially moving because the week before Mrs. Ferris had also written about Princess:

My pride an Joy

I went to sleep on New Year's Eve and I had an seizure but I couldn't come out of it but my dog pinces licked me. In the face an she kept hitting an hitting me in the face with her paws. When princes woke me she was still licking me. When I woke up princes was laying on my stomach. She knew something was wrong with me. She always know when something is wrong with me. I had her ever since an puppy. She save my life. I never been sick like this. That's why I call her my pride and Joy.

It was fascinating (and inevitable) how individual stories generated by the neighborhood photographs started to connect to the history of the community. The photographs of special places also revealed feelings about the community—an implicit yearning in the photo of a backyard fence with the John Hancock tower dim in the distance, a "scary" corridor, a building where "the ganglangers be selling their drugs," fond memories of a deceased parent, a previous residence that triggered a "good moment" from the past (see Figures 9.4 and 9.5).

The preponderance of neighborhood photographs expressed a sense of community pride. The neighborhood garden "lets you know we too have a green thumb." The photo of snow-shoveling janitors showed that they were not only doing a good job but also making sure the "kids will not hurt themselves." Carolyn Lee's photograph was of children walking safely to school because of her role as the crossing guard: "I be there every day because my 660 kids be looking for me."

A number of parents read aloud all or part of the piece they chose to be part of the Family History parent publication. Photographs, historic documents, and participants' writings were collected and consensus reached on how the publication would be distributed to participating families.

Pat brought along name books for people to research their name and their children's names. She also distributed construction paper and glue for people who wanted to turn their family tree worksheets into a more artistic and attractive document. "Write the name and relationship of each person on a leaf, then glue it to the appropriate branch of the tree. Roots should show place names and pathways to Chicago."

Before the final celebration, everyone took a few moments to assess the Family History Parent Project. Participants answered the following questions:

- How do you rate your participation in the Parent Project?
- What was your favorite part? Least favorite?
- What was your child's reaction to your work? Do you think it will help him/her?
- Would you like to continue meeting and working on family/community history?

In their evaluations of the Family History Parent Project, participants were unanimous in their enthusiasm to continue meeting. One parent wrote, "I love to talk about my life." Parents wrote that their children's reactions to their parents' participation in the project ranged from "shock" to "What is all this mess?" to

"Although we are all different, we are very much the same."

This Picture were taking by
the side of the abey.
Near My house. this is their
Little gard. where they
planting flowers and greens
grass. This let you know we
resident that live here in Cabrini
Green. we too have a green
thumb.

Marlene Scott

Figure 9.4   Marlene Scott's photograph and description of
a favorite neighborhood place.

Figure 9.5   Cheryl Savage's photograph and description of
her home in Cabrini-Green.

"My children think it's nice, because it helps them get into things that they're working on in school."

Clearly six weeks could not contain this project, so many avenues of inquiry had been opened to traffic. At Jenner School, two sets of parents completed the six-week workshop series—one in the fall and one in the spring. In the midst of this activity, family and community history continued to be recorded. In December, the principal, the parent coordinator, and the Parent Project facilitators wrote to Cook County Commissioner Jerry Butler, inviting him to give a guest presentation on his place in the history of the Cabrini-Green community:

> Our parents are taking part in this school-wide study and have been writing family histories, developing life time lines, and researching genealogical trees. They have studied newspaper articles and maps of the Cabrini-Green area from as far back as 1830, [including] the 1890's, the 1920's, up through the present. We are very proud that an accomplished person such as yourself is part of the history of this community.
> During your visit we would like you to describe the area where you grew up and answer questions posed by parents and students. . . . We are looking forward to hearing your story and claiming you again as part of our history.

Not all of the ongoing community, family, and personal histories were positive. There were tragic events as well. Rodger Hemphill, a much-loved member of the spring Family History Parent Project, was shot by a stray bullet shortly after the workshop series ended. Rodger survived. He was, ironically, the parent who had written about the gradual loss of the feeling of safety at Cabrini-Green in his character sketch of Ms. Carrie Ann Cade. Then, on January 9, 1997, a nine-year-old Jenner student and resident of Cabrini-Green was sexually assaulted, beaten, and left in a coma. It was a deeply disturbing event that sadly, yet necessarily, became part of the unfolding Cabrini-Green Family History Parent Project. Kathy Ellis recorded her response to the assault:

> My name is Mrs. Ellis, and I'm very hurt about what happened to ———. I remember when the child was first born. When the mother come from the hospital I hold her in my arms. What make it so bad is she live across the hall from me. When the mother have to go somewhere I will babysit all the kids for her and when she didn't have any food I will give her kids food to eat when they were hungry. Now I can't eat right or sleep. I volunteer at Jenner School and I work with the child everyday. She is just like my own child. . . . That all I been doing was crying.

Kathy Ellis standing in front of Family History Parent Project
artifacts, Jenner School, Chicago.

WHAT OTHERS ARE DOING

The *Journal of Ordinary Thought* (published by the Neighborhood Writing Alliance, 1313 E. 60th Street, Chicago, IL 60637, phone 773-684-2742) contains reflections people make on their personal histories and everyday experiences. Publishers describe the journal as "founded on the propositions that every person is a philosopher, expressing one's thoughts fosters creativity and change, and taking control of life requires people to think about the world and communicate the thoughts to others. *JOT* strives to be a vehicle for reflection, communication, and change." The June 1997 issue is entitled *The Father Issue* and contains family stories, personal reflections, and photographs. "By telling their own stories and speaking out on issues that affect them, the fathers hope to influence the attitudes and policies of society and its legislators" (p. 5).

Elementary teacher Rebecca Borjas (see Chapter 3) involves families of her second-grade students in "Stories from the Heart." A tape recorder is sent home and parents are invited to record a story from the past. Rebecca's second-grade students then share their family stories with a fifth-grade buddy class. The fifth graders typeset the family stories with a word processor, and the parents and their children then illustrate the stories. The final publication becomes an important personal and historical document—as well as a powerful learning experience for parents as well as their children and their fifth-grade buddies.

WHAT YOU CAN DO

Consider ways to integrate and enrich your classroom curriculum through family history. Encourage students to interview parents and grandparents as a regular part of classroom inquiry in all subject areas. Invite parents to come into class as "experts" to share their skills and knowledge. Support the telling and recording of family stories by arranging a Family Story Night, where parents record and publish favorite family memories. (A powerful and motivational read-aloud for Family Story Night is *Tell Me a Story, Momma* by Angela Johnson.)

RESOURCES

American Genealogical Research Institute Staff. 1973. *How to Trace Your Family Tree.* New York: Doubleday.

Emily Croom. 1994. *Unpuzzling Your Past: The Genealogist's Companion and Sourcebook.* Cincinatti, OH: Better Way Books.

Patrick Hanks and Flaria Hodges. 1990. *A Dictionary of First Names.* New York: Oxford University Press.

Elsdon C. Smith. 1973. *New Dictionary of American Family Names.* New York: Harper & Row.

Peter Stillman. 1989. *Families Writing.* Portsmouth, NH: Heinemann.

Jim Willard and Terry Willard, with Jane Wilson. 1997. *Ancestors: A Beginner's Guide to Family History and Geneology.* Boston: Houghton Mifflin.

Chapter 10

Parent Leadership: "It Doesn't Happen Just Because You Say So"

Sharing the "key to leadership" in the Parent-Teacher Leadership Project, Milwaukee.

*P*arent leadership is the key to family involvement in schools. Along with parent leadership come parent ownership, workshop agendas that truly reflect the interests and concerns of parents, program longevity, and the intellectual and emotional resources of the larger community. Parent leaders can significantly increase family involvement in any school—they can launch Parent Project workshops, help plan special community-school events, and make positive contributions to the general learning climate of the school. Many parents find another parent's voice authoritative, and parent leaders who are knowledgeable about curriculum can be especially helpful in explaining classroom practice and gaining other parents' support. Beyond the individual classroom and school, parent leadership is crucial to maintaining funding, developing other parent leaders, and institutionalizing the family-school connection.

In trying to build district-level parent leadership, it seems there are barriers at every turn—no money, no space, no way to identify participants, high rates of mobility. . . . These are, however, the same barriers that exist at the classroom level, so we decided to approach parent leadership the same way: through workshops in which participants have ownership of the agenda. The resulting Parent-Teacher Leadership Project was funded by the Helen Bader Foundation and co-led by Jacqueline Ward, who, you might recall from Chapter 7, is a parent activist and mother of two children in the Milwaukee public schools.

The guiding principles of the Parent-Teacher Leadership Project were these:

- Leadership is accomplished by doing rather than talking about doing.
- There are many different ways of providing leadership.
- Parent leaders can effectively train other parents to be leaders.
- It is generally not productive to separate parents from teachers—and this includes leadership training as well.

The project began in five Milwaukee public schools—three elementary and two middle schools. In our initial meetings with the principal, key staff representatives, and parents of each school, Jacqueline and I explained the goals and benefits of parent leadership. We asked each school to identify a team of five people. Ideally, this school team would be a mix of parents and teachers as well as the school's Parent Coordinator (if there was one). We asked team participants to commit to two different kinds of monthly workshops. The first would be with the four other school teams and would focus on leadership issues and strategies for implementing school-specific Parent Projects. The second monthly meeting would be at the individual school site and would serve to inform the rest of the school community about the project. Through the grant, we were able to offer participants stipends as a way of acknowledging the substantial time and work the Parent-Teacher Leadership Project would entail.

Jacqueline and I knew that in order for the project to be successful we needed to accomplish three things:

1. Build relationships between parents and teachers.
2. Support individuals in their feeling that they have something valuable to contribute.
3. Achieve meaningful and relevant results.

From our meetings with staff members from the individual schools, we understood that project participants would be culturally diverse and that perhaps up to a third would be primarily Spanish speakers. In order to accommodate the language and role differentials, we decided to begin the Parent-Teacher Leadership Project by involving the five school teams in the Milwaukee Public Schools' Ropes & Challenge course. As its title implies, "Ropes & Challenge" engages individuals in a physical struggle that can be overcome only through group physical effort and problem solving. Because Ropes & Challenge was also part of the Milwaukee Public School curriculum, it seemed like an especially appropriate way to begin building a sense of community and ownership.

The real challenge, however, proved to be more legal than physical—and considerably more time-consuming. Even though they were used by hundreds of teachers and students daily, the Milwaukee Public School system informed us that parents would not be permitted to use any Ropes & Challenge facility.

Finally, after weeks of delay, calls to Central Office, and a letter from the office of the Milwaukee City Attorney, Ropes & Challenge was officially opened to parents, as represented by the twenty-seven Parent-Teacher Leadership Project participants who were gathered together for the occasion. It was a symbolic moment. In general, school systems are not parent-friendly, and part of any leadership project, we now understood, would undoubtedly involve parents' simply gaining access to the system.

Guiding us on our initial Ropes & Challenge foray was Mark Schimenz, a counselor and father of two students at Grand Avenue Middle School. All of us met with Mark the day before we attempted the course itself as a way of preparing for the experience. Through this preparation we also began to learn more about each other, including names and biographical details.

While not as rigorous as Outward Bound, the Ropes & Challenge experience did provide plenty of physical exertion. Because of the legal and bureaucratic delays, it was now late fall, and we faced a day of icy wind and rain. Some of the Ropes & Challenge activities called on us to lift each other and form human chains of support. Although we were initially uncomfortable with the nature of some of the activities, they helped us cut through our language barriers while allowing us to better understand what it means to work together as a group.

For example, in "Island Rescue" all twenty-seven of us had to move from one elevated platform to another using two planks. The two planks together were of a length somewhat shorter than the distance between the two "islands." First, we had to solve the problem of the plank lengths and then decide how we were going to try to move everyone across—making sure we had a way to "rescue" the last person from the original, rapidly depopulating island. Actual execution of our "rescue" took a few tries, lots of teamwork, careful balancing, and physical support—lifting, pushing, pulling, and holding. People who criticize some group activities as "touchy-feely" would have to find new words to describe our Island Rescue. Yet it gave us a sense of accomplishment, community, teamwork—and we had fun. Translators in the group had emerged and we were beginning to sense different leadership styles.

The daylong Ropes & Challenge adventure led to our first group decision: to have Mark begin each of our subsequent monthly workshops with a Ropes & Challenge activity that would both get us involved in physical collaboration and help us focus on the workshop's particular agenda.

After the initial Ropes & Challenge experience, the location of the monthly leadership workshop rotated among the five schools. The host school was to be responsible for child care, refreshments, room arrangements, and a portion of the agenda. This hosting responsibility not only developed and strengthened the leadership abilities of the school teams, but also helped identify appropriate "parent space" within the individual schools.

We built the monthly leadership agendas from the issues and questions of participants: "Communication between parents and teachers." "Trust." "Barriers." "Definitions of parent involvement." "What does it mean to be a leader?" "Time management."

At the first leadership meeting, we identified a parent to send out invitations (in Spanish and English) to the subsequent meetings as well as keep track of names, addresses, attendance, and phone numbers (see the record-keeping forms in Appendix C). This secretarial and record-keeping work would be compensated by a stipend. The resulting monthly invitations

"We found out that when you have a difficult task to perform, you need to have a sense of humor. Everybody worked so hard, it was nice."

were personal, artistic, and inviting, containing information about location and time as well as the agenda for the next workshop session. The invitation to the February 14, 1997, workshop, for example, was a colorful Valentine's Day card. On the front, in the midst of cascading red hearts, was a quote from W. C. Fields: "My heart is a bargain today. Will you take it?" Inside there was a brief agenda for the next meeting, along with the location, time, and parking suggestions. Winged angels and garlands of hearts bordered the information.

It soon became apparent that school teams took pride in hosting the leadership workshops, and the refreshments and ambiance of the meeting rooms were increasingly impressive. From month to month attendance at leadership workshops actually increased. The monthly meetings became occasions to look forward to—a time for meeting friends, sharing ideas for family involvement, coming up with new ideas, and renewing our commitment to including more families in the education of their children.

The structure of each session consisted of an opening Ropes & Challenge community-building activity led by Mark, followed by a workshop that explored a specific leadership issue, led by the hosting school's team.

Leadership workshops used the same kind of methodology as other Parent Project workshops: they focused on writing, read-alouds, community-building activities, group work, and ownership of the agenda by all participants. Journals were distributed at our first meeting prior to the Ropes & Challenge adventure and became part of each successive workshop. Favorite read-alouds included the following:

Going Home by Eve Bunting and illustrated by David Diaz. Carlos and his family return to Mexico after a season working as farm laborers.

Abuela by Arthur Dorros and illustrated by Elisa Kleven. Rosalba and her grandmother fly over Manhattan.

Chrysanthemum by Kevin Henkes. "Chrysanthemum thought her name was absolutely perfect. And then she started school."

Author: A True Story by Helen Lester. The author of *Tacky the Penguin* writes about her struggles to become a writer.

Emma's Rug by Allen Say. Young Emma's artistic inspiration vanishes when her mother washes her prized possession: a small shaggy rug.

Too Many Tamales by Gary Soto. Maria tries on her mother's wedding ring while kneading the *masa*. The ring disappears and must be somewhere in the steaming batch of tamales.

In Daddy's Arms I Am Tall by Javaka Steptoe. Eleven African American writers celebrate fathers.

Working Cotton by Sherley Anne Williams. A poetic and disturbing day in the fields, told from the point of view of a young child.

LEADERSHIP WORKSHOP 1: WHAT IS PARENT INVOLVEMENT?

Holding onto the end of a large spool of purple twine, Mark unraveled enough to throw the spool across the room to Mimi. "Mimi!" he shouted as he made the toss. Mimi in turn held onto the twine and tossed the spool diagonally across the circle, shouting "Alex!" Alex made a very respectable one-handed catch. And so it went until the spool of purple twine came back at "Mark!" with everyone grasping their length of twine, which crisscrossed the circle like a purple spider web. "If we can't learn each other's name," Mark observed, "we can't accomplish our goals." Mark asked us to think about the ways each of us is connected to the group; the crossed lengths of purple twine provided a visual metaphor of how a community starts to form. Mark cut a length of purple twine for each person to keep as a reminder of the activity and the ways we are connected.

> *"Talk to me about how I can help my kids. Some practical information and ideas."*

"WHAT IS PARENT INVOLVEMENT IN SCHOOLS?" Hi-Mount parent Hope DeVougas wrote on chart paper. She asked each of us to spend a few minutes thinking about this question with our journal—writing, drawing, or both. "Parent involvement—for what? . . . What do you want and need for parents and families? Do you just want them in the building attending general functions? Or do you really want their help when it comes to educating their child? Do you want them working in the building, in the classroom, or even helping to make decisions on school policy, budget issues, hiring and evaluating teachers?" The questions Hope posed were crucial because how you define parent involvement determines what you get.

As individuals shared their definitions of parent involvement, they did so primarily by naming different kinds of activities. The activities ranged from helping their children with homework to participating in parent-teacher conferences to doing volunteer work at school to attending special school events to being elected to the school Site-Based Management Council to taking part in this very workshop.

The discussion focused on the different kinds of parent involvement there were and the kinds of support structures necessary to make them successful. One of the things that was made abundantly clear was the distinct nature of each school community. What worked in one school would not necessarily work in another. The other point we kept returning to was how essential parent leadership was to changing parent participation into more intentional and long-term involvement.

LEADERSHIP WORKSHOP 2: BARRIERS TO PARENT INVOLVEMENT

For our second workshop, the group met in the spacious library of the Milwaukee Education Center Middle School—which was fortunate because the opening Ropes & Challenge activity required a good deal of movement. As we sat in a large circle, Mark asked each of us to introduce ourselves and to name our children's school. Mark then said that we were going to be involved in an activity with a lot of symbolism.

Mark divided us into two groups: teachers/administrators and parents/ community. "We are going to have to cross a river," Mark said, pointing to a broad expanse of green library carpet. He passed out rubber circles about one foot in diameter to each of us. The circles were to be used to cross the river. The challenge was for each group to cross the river—stepping only on the rubber circles. The groups would start from separate areas in the library and then meet as one. At the spot where the groups converged there was a thin rope bridge, which we would have to cross single file. At the end of the rope bridge was a library table, which we would have to climb over.

It sounded simple, but movement over the rubber circles required planning and experimentation—not to mention a sense of balance and physical support from the persons in front and behind. Movement across the rope bridge involved even more balance and physical support.

After we had all helped each other over the final obstacle, the library table, we returned to sit in the large circle. Mark asked us to reflect on our "river crossing." Comments included the following:

- "Although we had made plans, the way we ended up crossing the river was nothing like the way we planned."
- "There was definitely a lot of support."

Mark asked us what the library table represented, especially in terms of what the group wanted to accomplish. "A barrier," we all agreed. "Just when you think you're finished and over the rope bridge," one parent observed, "there's another barrier to get over."

As he usually did at the conclusion of each Ropes & Challenge activity, Mark asked each of us to say a word or phrase to describe what we had learned from our river crossing; participants responded in English and Spanish.

"Comunidad."

"We all have to support each other."

"By the time we got to the rope bridge we weren't two different groups, but one."

"We went from 'us' to 'all.'"

"Together we stand, divided we fall."

"Unidad."

"Solidarity."

"Collaboration."

"Closeness."

"Equality."

"Connectedness."

"Amistad."

"Sticking together."

"Holding each other up."

"Friendship."

"We're united, together."

"All together for something better."

Finally Mark had us put the palm of our right hand down and the palm of our left hand up, connecting our circle. "We are not above anyone or below anyone here," he said. "We are all equal as we work for the well-being of children."

"I followed the signs to the Parent Center and it was locked!"

After refreshments, conversation, and some bookkeeping details (dealing with the sign-in sheet, checking addresses, etc.), the Hi-Mount school team facilitated a discussion of barriers to parent involvement. At the mention of barriers, we were reminded of how we felt as we helped hoist each other over the library table at the end of our river crossing.

Working in small groups, we compiled the following list of common barriers to parent involvement:

- Transportation
- Child care
- No telephone
- No extra money
- No place to live
- Not enough food
- Frustration
- Negative feelings or guilt feelings toward school(s)
- Timing (conflicts with work, dinner hour?)
- Not having productive things for parents and families to do
- Weather conditions
- Just plain tired

How do we overcome some of these barriers and make parent involvement work? The consensus seemed to be that part of the solution had to do with money and resources and part had to do with an ability to understand perspectives other than our own:

- Allocate sufficient money and resources.
- Plan events well (from a parent perspective).
- Consider times of events and meetings (from a parent perspective).
- Provide tasty refreshments for parents.
- Consider the content of the information being given: Does it involve the parents' children? Is it something that parents can use and take home?

LEADERSHIP WORKSHOP 3:
FROM MR. POTATO HEAD TO VIDEOTAPES

At the start of our third meeting, Mark asked us to sit at a table with five other people we didn't know well. Once at the table, we were to find someone in our group whose name we didn't know. "Introduce yourself to that person and find three unusual things you have in common," Mark said. "Then introduce your partner to the rest of the people at the table by sharing one of the three things you found you have in common."

After the introductions were done, Mark told us to close our eyes. He then gave each of the groups a package. Inside the package, he said, were parts belonging to Mr. Potato Head. With their eyes closed, members of each group were to assemble their Potato Head. In order to communicate with each other, we were to say our name before we spoke as well as the name of the person we were addressing. For example, "This is Mark speaking. Kathy, what part of Mr. Potato Head are you holding?" Part of the group process was to assemble Mr. Potato Head as well as communicate what he looked like to those who were encountering Mr. Potato Head for the first time.

After about ten minutes, we opened our eyes to view our strangely constructed Mr. Potato Heads. Mark asked each of us to think about something we learned from the process of doing this activity together. Here's what we had to say:

"We definitely needed to work together."

"It would have gone better if we had developed a plan of how we would work together."

"We all had to depend on the other person."

"I think everybody needs to work together to make something so hard."

"It would have gone better with our eyes open."

"Excuse me. Ours is a *Ms*. Potato Head."

"Even with our eyes closed, ours is color coordinated."

"Whatever we got, we love it anyway."

"It was a lot of fun doing this together."

"They say three or four hands are better than one—that's why ours has three hands."

"I learned everyone's name."

"Trust had to come into the process."

"We were shocked how good it came out. If we weren't sure what we were feeling, we would ask someone else to verify."

"We forgot about our names, but we felt each other's hands so we bonded very well."

Our Mr./Ms. Potato Heads put away, we turned to the primary workshop activity, which was for each school team to make a ten-minute videotape about their school. The audience of the videotape would be parents who wanted to know more about the particular school. The making of the videos would give individuals an opportunity to clarify what was really important about their school as well as support crucial leadership skills, such as public presentation.

School teams met to talk about what kind of video they would make. Kathleen Smith from Hi-Mount school gave each school team three questions to focus on:

1. What is the videotape going to look like?
2. Who is going to be on camera?
3. What are you going to say?

The Hi-Mount team had made their videotape in advance and played it for the rest of us as a kind of model of what works and what doesn't work. They also gave us advice from what they learned: "Don't write down every word you are going to say. Just use notes to remind you."

That we succeeded in planning, rehearsing, and producing the five videotapes in this one workshop meeting surprised everyone. It certainly would not have been possible without the extensive community-building activities that preceded it. Most school teams used the videotape as a way of introducing various school strengths and programs to their envisioned audience. In the Milwaukee Education Center tape, for example, the principal briefly described the history of the school and its educational philosophy, the parent coordinator discussed the various opportunities for parent involvement, and a parent explained how specific classroom instruction had helped motivate and prepare her children for high school and beyond.

Grand Avenue Middle School parents Gerry Howze and Cheryl Harris took a different approach, and assumed an audience of school administrators and teachers. They entitled their video "Parents' Perspective on Innovative Techniques to Create a Village at Our Schools." Gerry began the narration. "Schools are always thinking . . . 'How do we get the parents into the school?' How about, instead of trying to figure out ways of getting the parents *in*, we went to the homes to meet with the parents? That way there would be a chance for the parents to meet you, [for you] to find out what their interests are, and it would show an extra oomph of enthusiasm . . . that you are concerned about what their interests are and how you could possibly do something together." The camera then shifted to Cheryl, who discussed how important it was to praise parents. "At the beginning of the year we sent home with the children a Praise Letter for their parents, thanking them for all they've done in taking care of their children and sending them to Grand Avenue Middle School. The Praise Letter also invited families to a celebration, and therefore we started off connected."

LEADERSHIP WORKSHOP 4:
HOW DO YOU BECOME A LEADER?

Before our fourth meeting, Jacqueline and I asked Mark to design an activity that would help us focus on the importance of communication. Team participation in the Leadership Project had grown, and we were now working with about thirty participants. Mark had us stand in a close circle facing each other's backs. We were, Mark told us, about to experience the "Rainstorm" (see photo). The Rainstorm consisted of five sounds: (1) the palms of hands rubbing together; (2) fingers snapping; (3) feet tapping; (4) fingertips tapping the shoulders of the person ahead; and (5) palms tapping knees. We were to close our eyes and listen. Mark would initiate a sound and the person to his right would repeat it, and so the sound would go around the circle. When the sound returned to Mark, he would begin the next one. The activity was so relaxing that Mark finally had to stop people from continuing to tap on each other's shoulders, they liked it so much. As we experienced the Rainstorm, it no

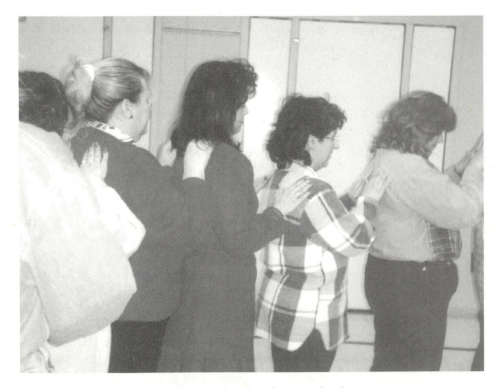

Listening to the Rainstorm at a Parent-Teacher Leadership Project, Milwaukee.

longer mattered that it was late Friday afternoon. When the Rainstorm was over, Mark led us in a discussion of the importance of listening and how it is an essential component of communication and leadership.

After the Rainstorm, school teams met to finalize their plans to increase family involvement in their respective school. Leadership, after all, is a process of doing, not talking about doing. The object was for each school team to design and implement a project that would connect families and schools in a meaningful, relevant way. In order to help schools realize their plans, each school team had $1,000 with which to leverage other funds and resources. As one parent commented, "If you want real parent involvement give us some money to spend." School teams needed to complete their $1,000 budget. Jacqueline and I distributed a Budget and Project Outline to help facilitate each school team's planning process. (Figures 10.1 and 10.2 are examples of completed forms; blank forms can be found in Appendix C.)

Parent Project Budget

School: _Albert E. Kagel Elementary School_

Project: _____

Amount		Person Responsible
$100 –	Child Care?	K. Hoppens
100 –	Materials and Supplies? Journals?	M. Foskett
300 –	Refreshments?	Parent volunteers
75 –	Transportation?	K. Hoppens
260 –	Stipends and Honorariums? _matched by Bilingual grant_	K. Hoppens
165 –	Publication and Celebration?	All committee members
0	Other (like custodian fees, security, field trips)?	n/a
$1,000	Total	

Figure 10.1   Leadership Project: sample budget.

Parent Project Outline

Goal of Project: Explore with parents various ways they can become active participants in their child's learning at the pre-school and elementary levels. Emphasis will be on skills specifically related to reading, writing, and speaking. Experiences will include exploring books, visiting bookstores, making books, and storytelling. A family interest and commitment to literacy will be created.

School: Albert E. Kagel Elementary School

How many participants? 30 families will participate. Both parents and children will participate in activities.
Where will project take place? Kagel's cafeteria.

Date and times of meetings? Six Saturday sessions beginning Feb. 21 from 10:00 A.M. to 12:00 P.M.
Who is responsible for each session? The seven committee members.

How will sessions be participatory and fun? Inspirational and motivational items will be distributed at each session. There will be hands-on activities for the parents at each session. At times there will be drawings or raffles. Guest speakers, storytellers will be invited. Refreshments will be served.

Will there be a final product for participants to share? (A book, a videotape, a celebration?) Each family will receive a certificate of completion. A family Polaroid photo will be attached. A book and/or storyteller doll will be created by each family.

What kind of evaluation? Survey of families with recommendations for future projects.

What do you need to do this project?

Figure 10.2   Leadership Project: sample outline.

Teams had been meeting at their individual schools monthly in order to decide on the focus of their respective projects. The final projects proposed by the five school teams reflected the unique needs of each school as well as the level of parent involvement already present.

- *School 1* decided to organize an environmental "greening" project to land-scape the vacant lot at the former site of Jeffrey Dahmer's apartment building. The vacant lot was part of the school neighborhood, and the land-scaping would coordinate with classroom greening and environmental curriculums.

- *School 2* decided on a family history project, in which each family would construct a square of a schoolwide family history quilt as part of the school's focus on family history.

- *School 3* would undertake a video project in which parents and their children would define for other parents what it means to keep a writing port-folio.

- *School 4* decided to set up a "Parents as Reading Partner" project in which parents would read a range of children's books, take field trips to book-stores and libraries, and work with a storyteller in order to write and pub-lish their own children's books. The concluding celebration of the project would feature family photographs and certificates of participation. (See Appendix C for sample certificates in English and Spanish.)

- *School 5* would organize a series of dinners in which teachers would spon-sor a table of their students' parents and then involve them in content-specific activities during the meal.

"Of course," one of the parents from Kagel School observed, "we have to take a poll of the parents before we finalize our plans or it isn't going to work."

This fourth session's workshop was conducted by the Kagel School team, and the focus was: How do you become a leader? "Leadership doesn't happen just because you say so," observed Kagel's assistant principal, Karen Hoppens. "How do you get from not being involved in school or just coming to parent conferences to actually being really involved in the school and being a parent leader? How do we get from A to Z?"

"What," the Kagel team went on, "do we mean by the word *leader*?" Then they recorded our responses: Listener. Motivator. Visionary. Sense of direction. Doer. Delegator. Commitment. Responsible. Assertive. Grant writer. Fundraiser. Then someone suggested crossing out the *d* of "fundraiser" to make it "fun raiser."

The ensuing discussion emphasized the point that people aren't leaders all the time. "Leadership is often situational, and when someone asks, 'How would you like to lead this or that?' it doesn't mean forever." It seemed important to lessen the pressure around the term "parent leader."

We counted off by numbers in order to form three groups different from our school teams. Each group was given a large sheet of paper containing an equally large drawing of a key. Groups were asked to "list activities and attitudes that assist in developing leaders." Each group was also to have a Scribe (to list the various attitudes and activities on and around the key), a Reporter (to explain the key to the whole group when we reassembled), and an Observer (to note leadership within the small group).

In my group a parent talked about how she gained leadership through opposition. Something was happening in her son's school that really bothered her, and she decided to try to do something about it. Through the process she found that she enjoyed being an advocate for parents. Almost everyone mentioned how important it was for schools to have a welcoming attitude and atmosphere.

When the whole group reassembled, we heard from the Reporters and Observers. The descriptions of leadership that emerged from the individual groups helped make us aware of the continual yet often subtle dynamic of leadership. For example, one Observer noted how much easier the group work became once the tasks were split up. Another Observer felt that "careful listening" was the first critical factor to developing leadership.

As we approached the conclusion of the Parent-Teacher Leadership Project, we began to assemble a Leadership Tool Kit—various resources that can be used in the operation, repair, and fine-tuning of individual school projects. Our tool kits contained the following items:

- Names and phone numbers of all Leadership Project participants.
- A list of community-building activities (see Chapter 4).
- An outline of a workshop format, a workshop checklist, and a sample letter to parents (see Appendix C).
- Blank sign-in attendance forms for participants, with spaces for name, address, home and work telephone numbers, and social security number (see Appendix C).
- Parent Project budget and outline forms (see Appendix C).
- A sign that says: DON'T FORGET TO TAKE A BREAK.
- A reminder of recurrent elements of Parent Projects (see Chapter 3).

- Copies of the invitations we mailed to participants during the year.
- A copy of the publication booklet from a previous Parent Project—for the enjoyment and encouragement of parents as they prepare their own publication (see sample parent-child collaborations in Chapter 3).
- A journal for personal writing, note taking, and planning.
- A copy of the videotape made by team members to introduce their school to other parents.
- A list of favorite read-alouds (Appendix B).

The most significant thing all of us learned from the year long Parent-Teacher Leadership Project was how leadership is achieved through the process of planning and doing. Give a group of committed people a budget and a goal that focuses on the academic success of their children and leadership will develop—in unexpected and impressive ways.

WHAT OTHERS ARE DOING

The Southwest Education Development Laboratory (SEDL) has been conducting long-term research related to parent involvement, parent involvement programs, and parent involvement networks. SEDL publishes excellent and concise research summaries, such as its "10 Truths of Parent Involvement" (see Appendix C). Truth number 7 is "Most barriers to parent involvement are found within school practices. They are not found within parents." (For the address of SEDL, see Appendix A.)

WHAT YOU CAN DO

Start. Start small, big, or in between. What is one thing you can do tomorrow to strengthen the connection between family and school, community and classroom? The projects in this book developed over time; you have the opportunity to set the clock ticking. How you create family involvement will be unique to you and your school and community. Take the next step, whatever it is, and continue to work with those who make family involvement in education a priority. Remember, leadership is a process of doing. Why not organize a family-school celebration?

Chapter 11
Celebrations

Families celebrate the completion of the Parent Project, Kagel School, Milwaukee.

When large numbers of parents gather together at their children's school, it is a time to celebrate learning and community. Donuts with Dad, Muffins with Mom, Family Story Night, Breakout with Bookmaking, Parents-as-Students Day, Sack-It-to-Me Saturdays, Coffee Chats with the Principal, Storytellers' Hour, Bring Someone Special to School Day. . . . Celebrations often occur on a monthly basis; the ability of a school to maintain and schedule such celebrations depends on whether they have identified and supported parent leaders.

What makes for a successful school celebration depends on the particular school community, but the following guidelines can contribute to a memorable celebration:

- Involve parents as well as community members (including business partners) in planning.
- Schedule events for a time that parents can attend. Parents need advance notice if the celebration takes place during working hours. Some schools publish a monthly newsletter that lists times and dates of events well in advance.
- Invite parents through individual contact as well as written notices. Remember, a generic flyer sent home with the homework could end up on the Bright Blue Bush. Make invitations attractive and parent friendly (written in the parents' first language). Ask parents to invite other parents. Hang up banners. Make schoolwide announcements. Put information about the event on the school's voice mail.
- Involve students in the planning of the celebration. As the "Trip to Cap Sauers" play demonstrates (Chapter 2), the best invitation for parent involvement is their child's enthusiasm.
- If there is no history of celebrations at your school, realize that it may take some extraordinary efforts to change attitudes and expectations.
- Make celebrations memorable. This usually means that children demonstrate learning for their parents or that parents and children become involved in a learning activity that extends into the family environment. Make it something that you yourself would want to participate in.
- Celebrate, don't lecture. If there is a formal presentation, keep it brief and connect it to an enjoyable interactive experience for parents, teachers, and children.
- Pay attention to the details in planning: coordinate food and supplies and make the meeting room(s) attractive. Don't skimp on the food.
- Start and end on time—especially if parents need to return to work.

- Learn from each celebration: What worked? What could be done better? Solicit feedback from participants, and listen carefully.
- Have expectations for participants. Plan to include some kind of structured, engaging interaction involving parents, children, and learning.
- Choose *quality* over *quantity* of events. Attendance at your next event will be only as good as the quality of the last one.
- Be positive and nonjudgmental; focus on how parents can support their children's learning.

Follow up with the parents who attend your celebration, and use these parents' input to build a program and an infrastructure that will expand and attract more parents over time. Offer workshops of interest to parents and of academic benefit for their children. Since parents' involvement in the education of their children occurs primarily outside of school, work together with parents to devise out-of-school or home activities that support classroom learning.

"I want teachers not to give up. To do the best they can do, and I'll do the same."

Chapter 12

Questions and Answers About the Parent Project

Parents celebrate publication of their writing at the conclusion of Family History Parent Project, Jenner School, Chicago.

Question: How much does a Parent Project cost, and where do you get your funding?

Answer: Parent Projects are quite inexpensive, especially if you consider the number of people who are affected—children, parents, and teachers. Costs generally include stipends, child care, materials, refreshments, and honorariums for guest speakers. A Parent Project budget can be as little as a few hundred or as much as a few thousand dollars. Major expenses are the stipends for participants and co-facilitators. Sometimes facilitators conduct the project as part of their job; sometimes stipends can be eliminated. Our funding usually comes from one of three sources: grants, school budgets, and Title I funds.

Question: Title I?

Answer: Title I is a federal program to help low-income students gain a quality education. Schools with a high percentage of low-income students receive Title I funds. Each school receiving Title I funds must have a parent involvement policy, and parents must have a say in how the school spends its Title I money. *School Districts that receive more than $500,000 of Title I money are required to spend* at least *1 percent of the total on parent involvement.*

Question: You spend a lot of time on community building. It looks like fun, but what happens when parents and teachers get impatient?

Answer: This happens, but not all that often. We explain the process at the beginning of any long-term project. Without forming a community, the group would have no longevity, no collective strength. In addition, when working with participants from diverse cultures and languages, community-building is crucial. At the end of each workshop's community building activities, we gather as a group and reflect on the experience and what the experience tells us about how we approach the project at hand—which is to form partnerships between parents and teachers.

Question: What's with all these baby books?

Answer: Picture books are now being used in the whole range of educational settings, including college, and the reason is that really good picture books appeal to all ages, like any work of literature. Using picture books for workshop read-alouds serves a number of purposes. Since our workshop time is limited, sharing a picture book allows for everyone to hear a story in its entirety, which is generally a satisfying experience in and of itself. Because we want to encourage parents to read with their children, picture books are especially useful because they allow us to easily demonstrate reading strategies. We always choose picture books that we think will appeal to parents. Often parents start bringing in their own favorites.

Question: How many teachers generally participate in a Parent Project? Are there instances in which no teachers take part?

Answer: Although parents can certainly work effectively without teacher participation, there are many reasons to include teachers—especially if you believe in parent-teacher partnerships. I think it would be intimidating for some parents if the majority of participants were teachers, however. Parent Projects generally have two or three teacher participants. Other teachers often give guest presentations. Successful Parent Projects have included equal numbers of parents and teachers. Specific proportions of parents and teachers are not as important as the climate of trust and the focus on children's learning.

Question: Have you any guidelines about whether or when children should also participate in workshops?

Answer: The best times to have children participate in a Parent Project workshop is when there is a productive and focused activity designed to involve parents *and* their children. Workshop activities and field trips that connect parents with the classroom curriculum are especially good times to invite parents to bring along their children. The final celebration of a Parent Project is also greatly enhanced by the presence of other family members.

Question: How have you incorporated technology into parent workshops?

Answer: Computer technology is one area many parents feel their children know more about than they do, so Parent Computer Projects have a built-in incentive for parents who want to level the playing field. Parents also have a strong interest in becoming computer literate, and many understand that an increasing amount of their interaction with their children and school will involve familiarity with a computer.

Dave Gawlik, a semi-retired computer specialist from Milwaukee's Hi-Mount School, has facilitated many Parent Computer Projects. When parents register for these projects, Dave asks them to complete a survey so that he can understand individual needs and computer knowledge (see Appendix C). A typical Parent Computer Project consists of six weekly two-hour workshop sessions.

At the first session Dave gives each participant a binder containing basic computer information, a disk, a sample keyboard, a notepad with pen, and a meeting schedule. During the following five weeks participants file additional computer information in the binder and use it as a writing portfolio. After personal introductions, the first workshop involves participants in putting pieces of a puzzle together on the computer screen as a way of familiarizing everyone with how to manipulate the mouse. Demonstrating on his own computer, the screen of which is projected onto a screen or wall, Dave shows participants how to make a personalized letterhead. At the second session parents use their personalized letterhead and the computer to compose a letter to someone who has made an important contribution to their lives. Those who are more experienced with computers mentor those who need help. Dave supplies stamped envelopes for the mailing of the printed letters. The third session involves parents in writing and mailing a second letter, this time to one (or all) of their children. The purpose of the fourth session is to show participants how to draw and paint using ClarisWorks so that everyone can design and print a personalized greeting card during the fifth workshop. During the sixth and final session, individual participants decide what they want to represent them in the computer Parent Project publication. Choices range from the greeting card, the two letters, or other writing, graphics, and illustrations produced during the project's six meetings. The opportunity to publish encourages all the participants to think of themselves as authors—and to understand the utility of the spell-check function. A read-aloud that humorously dispels computer anxiety is *Arthur's Computer Disaster* by Marc Brown.

Question: Six two-hour sessions sounds like heaven, but I don't have that sort of time available. Can I do successful parent involvement in a briefer time span?

Answer: Yes. Improving communication with parents does a lot to improve the climate necessary for parent involvement and can be accomplished in a number of time-efficient ways. Voice mail, newsletters, and open houses are just a few of the numerous opportunities for positive feedback and dialogue. The most time-efficient approach to parent involvement is to arrange a celebration of your students' learning (see Chapter 11). Developing a team of parent leaders, however, is more time-consuming, but is definitely worthwhile.

Question: What about Parent Projects in high school?

Answer: Toby Curry and Pete Leki have both been facilitating high school Parent Projects. Parents of high school students have fewer opportunities to interact with other parents and teachers than parents of elementary school students, and they greatly appreciate the chance to share and solve problems together. When high school parents construct their Parent Project agenda, many of their concerns focus on career and retention issues. The structure of high school Parent Projects remains the same: workshops are built from the interests of participants, read-alouds, home activities, the sharing of writing, and publication. The read-alouds in this case often consist of fewer picture books and more pieces that focus on adolescents. A particularly successful writing activity from the high school Parent Project conducted by Toby Curry and Jan Swenson invited parents to write a letter to their son or daughter: "What if you could only tell your kids ten things—what would be in your letter?"

Question: What can an individual teacher do?

Answer: You might try the Roving Parent Journal (Chapter 6). If you want to organize a group of parents for Parent Project workshops, you might begin by sending parents a survey to determine what they would like to see in terms of "parent involvement," then follow up by personally contacting the respondents. "Parent involvement" has to be one of your priorities, or you will eventually resent the time and energy it takes. Start with a small group of parents and build from there. Begin to network with other teachers and parents. Perhaps there's a community coalition with a parent focus that you can join. Document your successes and celebrate them with others. As Mark Schimenz would say, "Right palm down, left palm up. We are not above or below anyone here. We are all equal as we work for the well-being of children."

Appendix A
Publications and Organizations

PUBLICATIONS

Calkins, Lucy McCormick. 1997. *Raising Lifelong Learners: A Parent's Guide.* Reading, MA: Addison-Wesley.

> Using herself and her family as the basis for case studies, Lucy Calkins talks parent to parent about literacy, reading, writing, play, work habits, math, and scientific curiosity. The book includes appendixes by Lydia Bellino on such subjects as how to pick a preschool or kindergarten and what you should know about your school's curriculum. There is also a brief appendix entitled "The Importance of Parent Involvement."

Epstein, Joyce L. 1995. "School/Family/Community Partnerships." *Phi Delta Kappan* 76: 701–712.

> Epstein defines six categories of parent involvement: (1) preparing children for school; (2) communication from the school to the home; (3) parent presence in the school as volunteers, audiences, or workshop participants; (4) assistance with school learning activities in the home; (5) involvement in governance and advocacy; and (6) collaboration with community.

Fisher, Bobbi. 1998. *Joyful Learning in Kindergarten.* Portsmouth, NH: Heinemann.

> The section "Communicating with Parents" (pp. 137–143) gives examples of positive communication throughout the school year; subsections include "Starting the Year," "Ongoing Communication," "Parent Conferences," and a "Closing Celebration." An appendix contains a sample "Parents' Goals" form, a "Weekly Newsletter" template, and a "Parent Conference Planning" form. In another appendix are examples of a "Welcoming Letter to Parents" and forms for "Parents as Helpers," "Contributions from Home," and a "Letter to Parents Regarding the Lending Library."

Griswold, Karen, and Claudia M. Ullman. 1997. *Not a One-Way Street: The Power of Reciprocity in Family Literacy Programs.* Bronx, NY: Institute for Literacy Studies Lehman College.

> Through case studies this monograph defines the Family Literacy Involvement Through Education program located at Public School 40 in the Bronx, New York. Sections describe home visits, parenting workshops, staff development, the preschool classroom, and adult education classes.

Lareau, Annette. 1989. *Home Advantage: Social Class and Parental Intervention in Elementary Education.* New York: The Falmer Press.

> Lareau finds that upper-middle-class parents not only are better informed about schools but also are more comfortable in interacting with schools and teachers. Working-class families, in contrast, are often uncomfortable in schools and tend to regard education as the province of the school.

Myers, John, and Luetta Monson. 1992. *Involving Families.* Columbus, OH: National Middle School Association.

> This publication describes a ten-step program for establishing effective family involvement in middle schools (pp. 25–33): (1) assess needs; (2) hire a program coordinator; (3) match needs with resources; (4) educate teachers and school personnel; (5) recruit volunteers; (6) train volunteers; (7) coordinate the process; (8) systematize recognition and maintain morale; (9) publicize achievements; and (10) evaluate the program.

National Council of Jewish Women Center for the Child. 1997. *Parents as School Partners Dissemination Kit.* New York: National Council of Jewish Women Center for the Child.

> This organization's reports include: "A Critical Review of the Research Evidence"; a superintendent's survey of "Parent Involvement Policies, Programs, and Practices"; "Parent Focus Groups"; "Teacher Focus Groups"; "School Principal Focus Groups"; and a compilation of "Replicable Programs to Enhance Parent Involvement." The Center for the Child collaborates with the ERIC Clearing House on Urban Education at Columbia University to offer a nested web site and home page: http://eric-web.tc.columbia.edu/.

Parker, Diane. 1997. *Jamie: A Literacy Story.* York, ME: Stenhouse.

> The section "Connecting with Families" (pp. 25–32) documents a reader-response journal that parents and children keep together. Parker begins by inviting parents and children to a workshop in which she models the process, and then she asks parents to write journal entries twice a week about their child's response to the reading. Parker then reads and responds to the journals as they are returned to the classroom. "The journals became an important part of school life for at least two-thirds of our families" (p. 24).

Renihan, Patrick, and Frederick Renihan. 1995. "The Home School Psychological Contract: Implications for Parental Involvement in Middle Schooling." *Middle School Journal* 26: 57–61.

The article defines and explores the "stances" of parents toward schools and schools toward parents as "collaborative," "independent," and "adversarial." An understanding of these stances and how to negotiate between them should inform any systematic parent involvement program.

Routman, Regie. 1991. *Invitations: Changing as Teachers and Learners K–12*. Portsmouth, NH: Heinemann.

"Strong parent involvement is not a question of 'Should we?' but rather a question of 'How should we?'" (p. 485). Routman lists twelve suggestions for improving communication with parents (pp. 485–488) and in an appendix (pp. 103b–111b) reproduces various letters to parents, a sample parent newsletter, and a student newspaper for parents.

Swap, Susan McAllister. 1993. *Developing Home-School Partnerships*. New York: Teachers College Press.

Swap's book is a wide-ranging discussion of various approaches to parent involvement supported by succinct applications of research and scholarship. The chapter "Barriers to Parent Involvement" is particularly informative and provocative. To quote from that chapter: "Schools as they are traditionally managed do not seek or support parent involvement that is based on equal relationships, collaborative problem solving, regular self-evaluation, or open discussion of conflict. The result is an unsatisfying cycle in which most con-flict (even normal, useful conflict) is driven underground; the conflicts that do emerge tend to be explosive, threatening, and personalized; and the after-math of these explosions reinforces the need for ritualized management of home-school relations. Though honored by long tradition, this is a cycle and a system that is wasteful of energy, destructive of positive motivation, and ineffective in supporting children's growth" (p. 21).

Taylor, Denny, and Catherine Dorsey-Gaines. 1988. *Growing Up Literate: Learning from Inner-City Families*. Portsmouth, NH: Heinemann.

Winner of the 1988 Mina P. Shaughnessy Prize of the Modern Language Association, *Growing Up Literate* demonstrates the ways inner-city families use literacy for a range of purposes. The Shay Avenue families Taylor and Dorsey-Gaines document demonstrate literate lives that run counter to many popular media stereotypes. The section "School Literacy at Home" shows the importance of children's school experiences in daily family life. "Sex, race, economic status, and setting cannot be used as significant corre-lates of literacy. The myths and stereotypes that create images of specific groups (families who are poor, inner-city families, teenage mothers and their children) have no relevance when we stop counting and start observing and working with people" (pp. 201–202).

Vopat, James. 1994. *The Parent Project: A Workshop Approach to Parent Involvement.* York, ME: Stenhouse.

> A complete sourcebook for teachers, principals, and parent leaders that provides materials for conducting workshops with parents on writing, reading, self-esteem, and community building. The book documents how, using a workshop-process model, parents become involved with their children's classroom activities and are thus empowered to support their children's education.

Voss, Margaret M. 1996. *Hidden Literacies: Children Learning at Home and at School.* Portsmouth, NH: Heinemann.

> Focusing on three fourth-grade children, Voss demonstrates the crucial role family environment plays in developing literacy, and in the process makes a strong argument for teachers' understanding and valuing of the kinds of learning taking place in the home. There is also a discussion of the differences in the ways families from disparate socioeconomic levels interact with schools.

Winston, Linda. 1997. *Keepsakes: Using Family Stories in Elementary Classrooms.* Portsmouth, NH: Heinemann.

> This book explains how family stories can enrich the classroom curriculum. The author briefly describes a range of strategies for incorporating family history into the classroom, including parent-child storytelling workshops (pp. 37–41). Contains an extensive annotated bibliography of picture books.

ORGANIZATIONS

The **Chicago Panel on School Policy** publishes a number of reports aimed at improving public education in Chicago. The Chicago Panel also sponsors Parent Involvement Forums consisting of workshop sessions ranging from "Starting a Parent Center" to "What Parents of Special Education Students Need to Know" to "Understanding Your School's Budget." Workshops are led by teachers, parents, and school administrators. The Chicago Panel, 75 East Wacker Drive, Suite 300, Chicago, IL 60601.

The **Cross City Campaign for Urban School Reform** supports the work of reform leaders to create high-quality schools in urban areas. A primary focus of the Cross City Campaign is to reconnect schools with their communities. The organization publishes informative School and Community Working Papers. "Community and family members bring rich and diverse resources to the schools that are not available to the school acting in isolation. . . . Parents and family members provide another point of view of schools and education informed by their unique knowledge of their children and their role as their children's primary teachers" (Cahill, p. iii). Cross City Campaign for Urban School Reform, 407 S. Dearborn, Suite 1500, Chicago, IL 60605.

Designs for Change is a multiracial educational research and reform organization serving the fifty largest cities in the United States, with a particular emphasis on Chicago. According to one of its publications, "Designs for Change combines applied research and policy analysis with direct involvement in aiding reform." Among the organization's publications are *Building a School Community That Reads: A Resource Guide*, and *The Case for Parent and Community Involvement*. Designs for Change, 6 North Michigan Ave., Suite 1600, Chicago, IL 60602.

The **Southwest Education Development Laboratory** (SEDL), 211 East 7th Street, Austin, Texas 78701. See description in Chapter 10.

Appendix B

Favorite Read-Alouds

Balzola, Asun, and Josep MaParramón. 1986. *La primavera*. Hauppauge, NY: Barrons.

Baylor, Byrd. 1974. *Everybody Needs a Rock*. New York: Simon & Schuster.

Buchanan, Ken. 1991. *This House Is Made of Mud (Esta casa esta hecha de lodo)*. Flagstaff, AZ: Northland.

Bunting, Eve. 1996. *Going Home*. New York: HarperCollins.

Burton, Virginia Lee. 1942. *The Little House*. Boston: Houghton Mifflin.

Brown, Marc. 1997. *Arthur's Computer Disaster*. New York: Little, Brown.

Browne, Anthony. 1984. *Willy the Wimp*. New York: Knopf.

Cisneros, Sandra. 1991. *The House on Mango Street*. New York: Vintage.

———. 1994. *Hairs = Pelitos*. New York: Knopf.

Clements, Andrew. 1992. *Billy and the Bad Teacher*. New York: Simon & Schuster.

Cohen, Miriam. 1980. *First Grade Takes a Test*. New York: Dell.

dePaola, Tomie. 1988. *La Leyenda del Pincel Indio*. New York: Putnam & Grosset.

Dorros, Arthur. 1991. *Abuela*. New York: Dutton.

Frasier, Debra. 1991. *On the Day You Were Born*. New York: Harcourt Brace.

Henkes, Kevin. 1991. *Chrysanthemum*. New York: Mulberry.

Hiscock, Bruce. 1997. *The Big Rivers*. New York: Atheneum.

Jessel, Tim. 1994. *Amorak*. Mankato, MN: Creative Education.

Johnson, Angela. 1989. *Tell Me a Story, Mama*. New York: Orchard.

Kraus, Robert. 1971. *Leo the Late Bloomer*. New York: Windmill.

Lester, Helen. 1997. *Author: A True Story*. Boston: Houghton Mifflin.

Meyers, Walter Dean. 1993. *Brown Angels*. New York: HarperCollins.

Orozco, José-Louis. 1997. *Diez Deditos (Ten Little Fingers)*. New York: Dutton.

Ringgold, Faith. 1992. *Aunt Harriet's Underground Railroad in the Sky*. New York: Dragonfly.

Say, Allen. 1996. *Emma's Rug*. Boston: Houghton Mifflin.

Scieszka, John. 1995. *Math Curse*. New York: Viking.

Sollman, Carolyn. 1994. *Through the Cracks*. Worcester, MA: Davis Publications.

Soto, Gary. 1993. *Too Many Tamales*. New York: Putnam & Grossett.

Steptoe, Javaka. 1997. *In Daddy's Arms I Am Tall*. New York: Lee & Low.

Williams, Sherley Anne. 1992. *Working Cotton*. New York: Harcourt Brace.

Appendix C

Workshop Materials

Rebecca Borjas's Home Visit Letter (in English and Spanish)

Rebecca Borjas's Home Visit Interview Form

Family Tree Data (for Self)

Family Tree Data (for Relatives)

Family Tree

Parent Project Budget

Parent Project Outline

Parent Project Checklist

Sample Parent Project Letter

Running a Parent Workshop: A Sample Schedule

Sample Attendance Record Sheet

Certificates of Participation (in English and Spanish)

Ten Truths of Parent Involvement (in English and Spanish)

Dave Gawlik's Parent Computer Project Registration

Rebecca Borjas's Home Visit Letter

Dear Parents,

     This year I hope to visit each child in his or her home. By making a home visit I will get to know you and your child better. By doing this I will be better able to understand your child and help him or her be successful in school. My goal is to make the children's education as meaningful as possible. Visiting in your home gives me ideas on how to do this. Visits will last for half an hour. Please fill out the bottom portion of this notice and return it to school with your child.

     Thank you for your support. Together we can ensure the best education for your child.

     Sincerely,

_____

The best time for a visit is:

Weekdays:

_____ 2:30–5:00 P.M.   _____ 6:00–7:30 P.M.

Saturday:

_____ A.M.   _____ P.M.

This would be a good date for me: _____

Student _____

Parent _____   Phone _____

Address _____

Comments:

Rebecca Borjas's Home Visit Letter

Estimados Padres,

Este año espero visitar a cada niño en su hogar. La visita me ayudará a conocerlos mejor. Por medio de esta visita podré ayudar a que su hijo/a tenga éxito en la escuela. Mi meta es que la educación de su hijo sea significante. Las visitas en casa me ayudarán a lograr esto. La visita será de media hora. Por favor complete la parte de abajo y devuelvala al la escuela mañana con su hijo.

Gracias por su apoyo. Juntos podremos asegurar la mejor educación para su hijo.

Sinceramente,

La mejor hora para la visita es:

lunes a viernes:
_____ 2:30–5:00 P.M.   _____ 6:00–7:30 P.M.

sábado:
_____ por la mañana   _____ por la tarde

Este es un buen dia para mí: _____

Alumno _____

Padre _____ Teléfono _____

Domicilio _____

Comentario:

Rebecca Borjas's Home Visit Interview Form

Student _____ Date _____

Place of birth _____ Age _____ Pet _____

Special interests _____

Siblings/ages _____

Mother _____ Place of birth _____

Occupation _____ Duties _____

Hobbies/special interests/musical instrument _____

Father _____ Place of birth _____

Occupation _____ Duties _____

Hobbies/special interests/musical instrument _____

Traditions and Family Customs

Stories _____

Songs _____

Special words/sayings _____

Games _____

Celebrations _____

Foods _____

Favorite family outing/activity _____

Others living in the home _____

Travels _____

Possible curricular connections _____

_____

_____

Notes/Comments:

Family Tree Data (for Self)

Name:
Date and place of birth:
Date and place of marriage:

Name of your spouse:

Brothers and sisters:

Your children:

Your occupation:

Places you have lived:

Questions:

Stories, memories, and interesting facts:

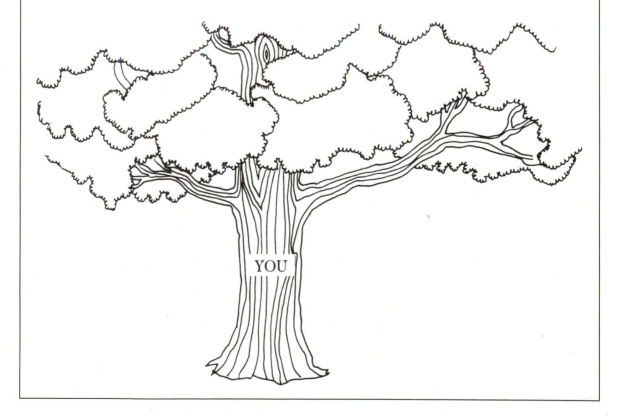

Family Tree Data (for Relatives)

Name:
Date and place of birth:
Date and place of marriage:
Date and place of death:
Occupation:

Questions:

Stories and interesting facts:

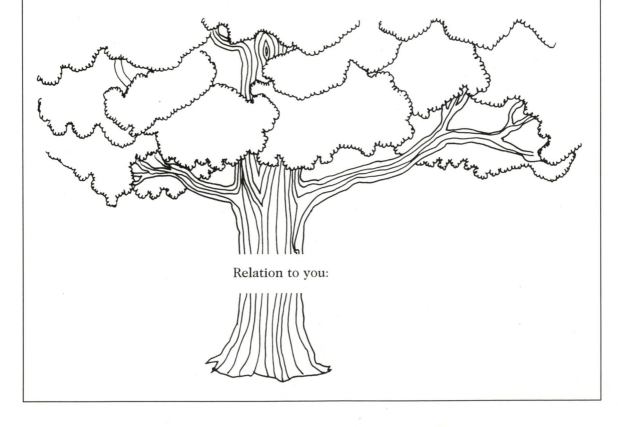

Relation to you:

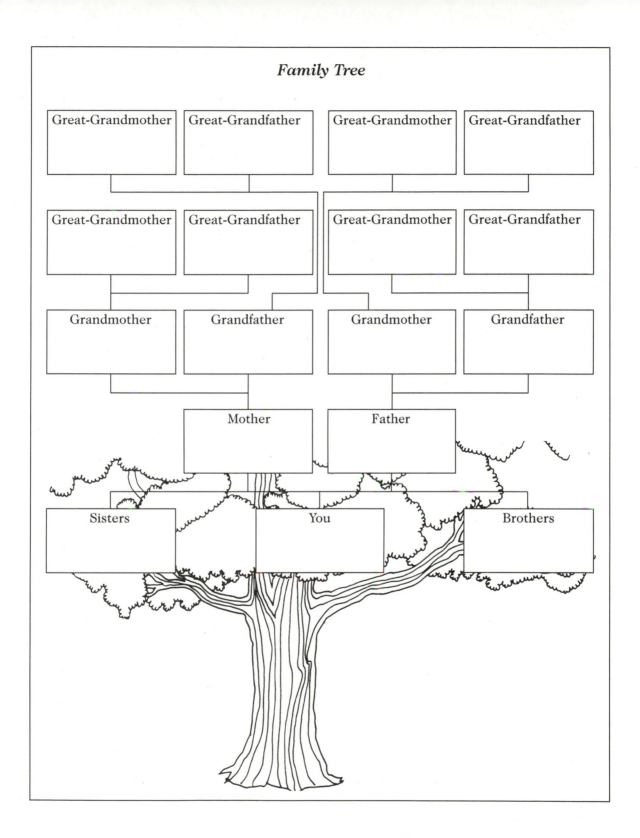

Family Tree

Great-Grandmother

Great-Grandfather

Great-Grandmother

Great-Grandfather

Great-Grandmother

Great-Grandfather

Great-Grandmother

Great-Grandfather

Grandmother

Grandfather

Grandmother

Grandfather

Mother

Father

Sisters

You

Brothers

Parent Project Budget

School: _____

Project: _____

Amount		Person Responsible
_____	Child Care?	_____
_____	Materials and Supplies? Journals?	_____
_____	Refreshments?	_____
_____	Transportation?	_____
_____	Stipends and Honorariums?	_____
_____	Publication and Celebration?	_____
_____	Other (like custodian fees, security, field trips)?	_____
_____	Total	

Parent Project Outline

Goal of Project:

School:

How many participants?

Where will project take place?

Date and times of meetings?

Who is responsible for each session?

How will sessions be participatory and fun?

Will there be a final product for participants to share?

What kind of evaluation?

What do you need to do this project?

5 . . . 4 . . . 3 . . . 2 . . . 1 . . . *Parent Project Checklist*

_____ Reminder sent to all participants confirming workshop dates, time, and place.

_____ Speaking of "place," do you need a building permit?

_____ If you need a building permit, then you probably also need to clear things with the building engineer.

_____ Agreement or commitment forms. Other attempts to make participants feel "invited."

_____ Phone reminders to participants and guest speakers.

_____ Food and drink for break. Who is setting up?

_____ Guest presenters—do they need any special equipment?

_____ Child care—including place, personnel, snacks, and materials.

_____ Security concerns for workshops held after school and in the evening.

_____ Attendance sheet of some sort if paying stipends. (Passing a sheet of paper around and having people "sign in" is still the best.)

_____ There is shared responsibility. No one person should try to be responsible for all these items.

Sample Parent Project Letter

Dear Parents,

     Some parents in the Parent Project expressed an interest in learning more about computers; therefore, we are offering a beginning computer class for parents starting Monday, February 10, from 4:00 P.M. to 6:00 P.M. We will always begin *promptly at 4:00 P.M.* so that we are able to make the best use of our time together.

Our classes will occur as follows:

Monday, February 10
Monday, February 17
Monday, March 2
Thursday, March 5
Thursday, March 12
Monday, March 16

Child care will be available. Classes will be held in room _____ at _____ School.

We are looking for parents that are interested in a full six-week commitment to the project. If you are interested in joining us, please return this sheet to the above address by Thursday, February 6.

_____ I will be able to attend on a weekly basis and will be available at 4:00 P.M.

_____ I will not be available to attend, but please keep my name on the list for future classes.

Name _____

Address _____

Zip _____

Phone _____

Best time to call _____

Running a Parent Workshop: A Sample Schedule

We find it most productive to schedule two-hour workshops. This gives enough time to have some introductory follow-up from the last week's workshop, a guest presentation, and some meaningful application.

Who's Here, Why Are We Here, and What's Happened Since We Last Met (30 minutes)

It is extremely important to "re-form" the group every time it meets. For us, this usually involves a warm greeting, a preview of the evening's focus, and then a welcome round in which individuals introduce themselves, give the names and ages of their children, and relate some comment or observation about the previous week's Parent Project activity. If we have extra time, we ask parents and teachers for any school news from the previous week.

Guest Presentation (30 minutes)

Parents and teachers enjoy hearing from experts on topics immediately relevant to their own lives and their hopes (and fears) for their children: fire safety, lead poisoning, the new math, self-esteem, journal writing, scribble stories, child development. At best, the guest presentation fits into the evening's workshop focus and generates interactive discussion and/or a hands-on activity. We all sit around a circle together, and we encourage our guests to see themselves as workshop participants as well. We discourage lecturing and try to see the guest presentation as having room for conversation and interaction. One memorable guest presentation, for example, involved a student teacher from the school showing the parents how they could use creative dramatics at home by actually doing six activities with them. There would have been universal disappointment if the student teacher had spent her entire time telling us about creative dramatics instead of letting us do them. We invite all guests to stay for the entire two hours of the workshop and to participate as fully as they can.

Break (10 minutes)

The break is sometimes the most crucial Parent Project time. It allows for socializing as well as spontaneous small-group discussions between parents and teachers. If the workshop takes place in the late afternoon, say 4:00 P.M. to 6:00 P.M., then we try to provide coffee, soda, and some substantial food (sandwiches, pizza, or salad). If the workshop is held after dinnertime, say 6:30 P.M. to 8:30 P.M., then we try to provide coffee, soda, and some cookies.

Regroup and Discussion of Guest Presentation (40 minutes)

At this point, we are interested in how parents and teachers individually respond to the guest presentation and how they can apply what they have observed to home and classroom. Usually we break into small groups of three or four and then report back and discuss in the large group toward the end. This is a good time for sharing children's books, writing in journals, and listening to classroom news from the teachers.

Assignment for Next Week, Wrap-Up, and Bolt for the Door (10 minutes)

Everyone needs to agree on some practical application of the evening's workshop to try out during the week at school or home: for example, "catching" your child doing something good after the self-esteem workshop; checking a book out of the library with your child after the library "field trip"; reading your story to your child and having him or her illustrate it with a self-portrait after the writing workshop. We will then begin the next week with our observations about how this activity has worked.

Whether the workshop ends at 4:30 P.M. or 8:30 P.M., it has, for parents and teachers alike, been a very long day. Wrapping things up and planning a new activity is a nice way to end it though.

Sample Attendance Record Sheet

Days Present	Last Name	First Name	SS#	Telephone	School

Certificate of Participation

Presented to:

_____

Their child:

_____

for their participation in the Parent Project at

_____

Given this _____ day of _____, 19_____.

Certificado de Participación

Presentado a:

_____

y sus hijos:

_____

por su participación en el Projecto de Padres de

_____

Reconocidos este _____ día de _____, 19___.

_____

Ten Truths of Parent Involvement

1. *All parents have hopes and goals for their children.*
   They differ in how they support their children's efforts to achieve those goals.

2. *The home is one of several spheres that simultaneously influence a child.*
   The school must work with other spheres for the child's benefit, not push them apart.

3. *The parent is the central contributor to a child's education.*
   Schools can either co-opt that role or recognize the potential of the parent.

4. *Parent involvement must be a legitimate element of education.*
   It deserves equal emphasis with elements such as program improvement and evaluation.

5. *Parent involvement is a process, not a program of activities.*
   It requires ongoing energy and effort.

6. *Parent involvement requires a vision, a policy, and a framework.*
   A consensus of understanding is important.

7. *Parents' interaction with their own children is the cornerstone of parent involvement.*
   A program must recognize the value, diversity, and difficulty of this role.

8. *Most barriers to parent involvement are found within school practices.*
   They are not found within parents.

9. *Any parent can be "hard to reach."*
   Parents must be identified and approached individually; they are not defined by gender, ethnicity, family situation, education, or income.

10. *Successful parent involvement nurtures relationships and partnerships.*
    It strengthens bonds between home and school, parent and educator, parent and child, school and community.

Reprinted by permission of the Southwest Educational Development Laboratory (SEDL)

Diez Principios Sobre la Participación de Padres

1. *Todos los padres de familia tienen esperanzas y metas para sus hijos.*
   Hay diferencias en la medida en que los padres apoyan los esfuerzos de sus hijos para lograr esas metas.

2. *El hogar es una de varios "mundos" que tienen gran influencia sobre el niño.*
   Para beneficiar al niño, la escuela debe trabajar en concierto con estos otros "mundos," no en oposición.

3. *Los padres desempeñan el papel principal en la educación de sus hijos.*
   La escuela puede reconocer y apoyar a los padres en esa tarea, o negarles su lugar.

4. *La participación de los padres debe ser una parte íntegra del sistema educativo.*
   Merece igual importancia que otros elementos, tales como "el mejoramiento del programa educativo" y "la evaluación."

5. *La participación de los padres es un proceso, no solo un programa de actividades.*
   Esto requiere energía y esfuerzo constante.

6. *La relación mutua de padres e hijos sirve como fundamento para la participación.*
   El programa debe reconocer el valor, la diversidad y la dificultad de esa relación.

7. *La participación de los padres requiere visión, estructura, y dirección.*
   Un entendimiento común es importante.

8. *La mayoría de los obstáculos que impiden la participación de los padres se encuentran dentro de las escuelas.*
   No en los padres.

9. *Cualquier padre de familia puede tener dificultades en participar.*
   Se debe de tratar a los padres como individuos: no se definen por género, raza, situación familiar, educación, o nivel de ingresos.

10. *Un buen programa de participación de padres promueve la colaboración y las buenas relaciones.*
    Fortalece los lazos entre el hogar y la escuela, padres y educadores, la escuela y la comunidad, y entre padres e hijos.

Dave Gawlik's Parent Computer Project Registration

Name _____

Address _____

Phone number and best time to call _____

Children's names, room, and grade _____

_____

_____

Have you used a computer before? _____

_____

What would you like to learn about in the next few weeks?____

_____

_____

Do you need to use computer skills in your job now or in the future?____

_____

_____

Please remember to sign in when you arrive each week. Thank you.

Works Cited

Austin, Terri. 1994. *Changing the View: Student-Led Parent Conferences.* Portsmouth, NH: Heinemann.

Cahill, Michele. 1996. *Schools and Community Parterships: Reforming Schools, Revitalizing Communities.* Chicago: Cross City Campaign for Urban School Reform.

Clark, Reginald. 1990. "Reformers Awaken to Parents' Role." In Maudlyne Iherjirika, ed., *CATALYST–Voices of Chicago School Reform 2,* 1 (September).

Daniels, Harvey. 1994. *Literature Circles: Voice and Choice in the Student-Centered Classroom.* York, ME: Stenhouse.

Department of Education. 1996. "America Reads" Challenge.

Hill, Bonnie Campbell, et al., eds. 1995. *Literature Circles and Response.* Norwood, MA: Christopher-Gordon.

Peterson, Robert. 1998. "Motivating Students to Do Quality Work." *Rethinking Schools* 12, 3 (Spring).

Renihan, Patrick, and Frederick Renihan. 1995. "The Home-School Psychological Contract: Implications for Parent Involvement in Middle Schooling." *Middle School Journal* (January): 57–61.

Routman, Regie. 1991. *Invitations: Changing as Teachers and Learners K–12.* Portsmouth, NH: Heinemann.

The Parent Project

A Workshop Approach to Parent Involvement

James Vopat

1994 • 248 pp/paper • 1-57110-001-6

Parental involvement strengthens the link between home and school. To achieve this goal parents need to be introduced to the revitalized classroom. Using a workshop/process model, parents become involved with their children's classroom activities and support their children's education. The workshops ensure participant ownership of a program's overall agenda while providing long-term structures for support and continued development.

Developed in urban bilingual school settings, *The Parent Project*

- provides a framework for implementing ways to get parents involved and informed;
- is the first book to connect parents with progressive education and changes in today's classrooms;
- is a complete source-book for teachers and principals that provides materials for conducting workshops with parents in writing, reading, self-esteem, and community-building;
- provides a detailed description of what the workshop approach is and how it functions.

Includes reproducible workshop handouts and formats in Spanish and English.

The Bridge to School
Entering a New World

Liz Waterland
Foreword by Glenda L. Bissex

1995 • 88 pp/paper • 1-57110-020-2

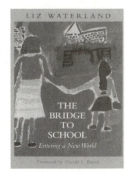

For some children, starting school is an adventure full of inconsistencies and contradictions between the world of home and a new world of expectation and strangers. For a parent, a child's first days of school recall a mixture of memories and bring up a host of concerns for the child's success. For the principal, the new school year presents many delicate decisions and tests her skills at meeting the needs of tentative children and questioning parents.

Aware that she needed to gain a better understanding of the experiences that school offers its children, parents, and staff as they begin the new school year, Liz Waterland spent three months researching, observing, and recording what she saw and heard. These written, taped, and remembered notes became *The Bridge to School,* an imaginative reconstruction of several months in the life of a school. She writes, "We cannot ask small children to make sense of the world of school unless we have stepped into it with them. We need to bend our backs to their eye level and wonder what it is that we see. We need to listen to the voices and words that children hear as if they are a foreign language. We need to feel fears and joys that are long lost to us, or that we may never have known."

Methods that Matter
Six Structures for Best Practice Classrooms

Harvey Daniels and Marilyn Bizar

1998 • 272 pp/paper • full-color insert • 1-57110-082-2

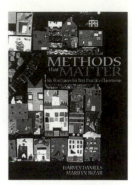

Harvey Daniels and Marilyn Bizar identify six basic teaching structures that will make your classroom more active, experiential, collaborative, democratic, and cognitive, while simultaneously meeting the emerging standards of "Best Practice" across subject areas and through the grades.

- Integrative units—extending thematic, interdisciplinary inquiries co-planned with students, drawing on knowledge and skills from across the curriculum.
- Small group activities—structuring collaborative pairs, groups, and teams that decentralize the classroom and individualize the curriculum.
- Representing-to-learn—engaging ideas through writing and art; exploring genres and media of expression as ways of investigating, remembering, and applying information.
- Classroom workshop—applying the studio-apprenticeship method with teacher modeling and coaching, student choice, responsibility, and exhibition.
- Authentic experiences—curriculum-centered ways of bringing life into school and students into the community for research and service.
- Reflective assessment—nurturing student reflection, goal-setting, and self-assessment; widening the evaluative roles and repertoires of teachers and parents.

For information on all Stenhouse publications please write or call for a catalogue or visit our web site at **www.stenhouse.com**.

Stenhouse Publishers
P.O. Box 360
York, ME 03909
(800) 988-9812